GRAYLING

GRAYLING

R.V. RIGHYNI

SWAN·HILL
PRESS

Copyright © 1968 R. V. Righyni

First published in the UK in 1968
by Macdonald and Company (Publishers) Ltd

This edition published 1996
by Swan Hill Press, an imprint of Airlife Publishing Ltd

British Library Cataloguing in Publication Data
A catalogue record for this book
is available from the British Library

ISBN 1 85310 778 6

Typeset by Hewer Text Composition Services Ltd
Printed in England by Livesey Ltd, Shrewsbury

Swan Hill Press

an imprint of Airlife Publishing Ltd
101 Longden Road, Shrewsbury SY3 9EB, England

Contents

Editor's Introduction

It is a fault of human nature to wish to classify, and it is unfortunate for the grayling that it has always resisted classification. It belongs to the salmon family, but refuses to conform to the breeding time of others in the same group. Trout fishers catch it and curse it when it is in its worst possible condition; when it is at its best, many of those who fish for trout in the spring and summer are banging away at pheasants and partridges.

The grayling has therefore come to be regarded in many waters as undesirable vermin, which is a great pity because it is one of the most beautiful and sporting of all fish, and excellent eating into the bargain. Its habits encourage fishing for it by some of the most pleasant and enjoyable of all angling methods, fly-fishing and light float fishing, and it is therefore not at all surprising that it should have attracted the attention of Reg Righyni, who is primarily a notable trout and salmon fisher. His book is the first for many years to deal with grayling, earlier classics by Pritt, Walbran, Rolt and Carter Platts having appeared before many modern tackle developments like nylon lines and fibre glass rods were available. It is a very worthy successor.

RICHARD WALKER

When the manuscript of this book was completed I asked Major Oliver Kite to peruse the sections where his name was mentioned and let me know if he disapproved of anything I had said. Characteristically he replied immediately saying that I was free to write anything I wished about him. Later, having read the pages, he wrote 'Don't alter a word, not even a comma'.

Oliver's tragic death on 15th June 1968 took place before the final printing of the book and my references to him are now sadly in the wrong tense. But I feel that all will agree with my decision that the lines should nevertheless appear exactly as Oliver saw them.

Preface

Many anglers put their rods away at the end of the trout season. Their attitude to the grayling varies. Some do no more than passively ignore this handsome member of the salmon family. Others vehemently make known their belief that the grayling cannot possibly create fishing interest in any way comparable with trouting.

I know from experience that no words of mine can make any impression on those who have turned their minds against the grayling. My mention of them is for another purpose. It is to show the young angler and the novice the need to make their own judgment of grayling fishing from personal trials. To allow themselves to be denied this splendid sport purely on the grounds of the views of the disparagers could be most regrettable.

Once the newcomer can reflect on a few hours of October dry-fly fishing, crammed non-stop with intriguing incidents, or the gyrating fight of a powerful December grayling at the end of a long, fine, float-fishing line, he can make his own inviolate decision. If this is to proceed with grayling fishing, he will find himself in good company, whether it be on North Country rivers or chalk streams.

It is surely significant that some of the finest trout fishers are devotees of grayling fishing. And no matter how the individual enthusiast may make his personal comparison between fishing for grayling and other game fish, he is certain to agree that, on suitable days in autumn and winter, the grayling provides most contenting enjoyment.

What more can be asked of a fish?

Getting to know Grayling

For many years my grayling fishing was restricted to the Wharfe, Yore, Swale, and one or two neighbouring Yorkshire streams. From time to time I had tempting ideas of trying some of the famous grayling rivers further afield. But so good and pleasing was my home ground that 1939 and the army days came before any new grayling adventure had got beyond the wishing stage.

All the grayling from the familiar waters looked very much alike to me. There were differences in hue – some golden, some steely and others lilac. Occasionally one was very slightly plumper than average. But all were of the same basically firm, slender type – all very beautiful: indeed, perfect to my eye.

Shortly after the war 'Tommy' Tomkin suggested a couple of days on his beloved Dove and the Manifold, and soon I caught my first Derbyshire grayling. It came from the Dove, just a hundred yards or so above the point where it is joined by the Manifold. It was a splendid fish: a little deeper and relatively heavier than I had known before, but otherwise I noticed nothing unusual.

I fished my way down to the junction, and then went a few yards up the Manifold. In no time there was a grayling in the net and I was very impressed by its pinkish hue. As I unhooked it I was struck by what I thought was a most peculiar formation of the mouth and assumed that it was a freak. The upper jaw was very much overshot and protruded well below the lower jaw, giving it a beak-like appearance. An inch or so away, on the underside of the fish, there was a bulge that looked like a little crop. I thought I must make a point of showing this apparently odd creature to my friend.

Within a cast or two, another grayling was giving me a stubborn fight. On landing it, I was surprised to find that it was identical to the former one. In a short, very busy time, I had a nice basket of fish. All those from the Manifold were similar and I realised that this, to me peculiar, appearance must be a common feature in this water.

That evening in the hotel named after the most famous of all anglers, I sat in the room – then very little changed from its original form – where Izaak Walton in person used to relax and take his glass after his days on the Dove. The enchantment of the occasion was very, very real to me. I had the thought that in this present very different age, a quiet winter day on a grayling stream probably retains more of the atmosphere of Izaak Walton's times than any other kind of fishing.

The grayling being so high in my esteem, I naturally looked at any photographs or pictures of the species particularly carefully. Eventually I saw some beautiful paintings of fish by Bernard Venables, and my eye lingered on the grayling. I blush to say it – blush is not nearly strong enough – but I wrote to the famous author-artist to tell him that he had got the dorsal fin wrong. He had painted the trailing edge as a lobe-like curve from the upper edge to the root. I said quite unequivocally that it ought to be very angular and pointed.

Bernard replied saying that Kennet grayling are like the one he had painted. 'Come and catch some and see for yourself' he said; and I did.

Small grayling from this magnificent chalk stream are very similar to those elsewhere. The bigger fish are extremely portly compared with Yorkshire grayling and the rounding of the dorsil fin appears to be a development which comes as the fish matures. The relative thickness of the body extends right to the tail and I should think that a good sized Kennet fish is as heavy for its length as any grayling can be.

Bernard and I had some interesting discussions about the unusual pointed leading edge of the pupil of the grayling's eye. We agreed that this probably gives the fish increased power of vision at very close quarters, which could perhaps account for some of their peculiar antics with the artificial floating fly.

It now began to sink in how ignorant I had been of the variations that could exist in grayling. I became anxious to see specimens from new places, and jumped at the chance when Arthur Oglesby and Eric Horsfall Turner invited me to fish the upper Yorkshire Derwent and an East Yorkshire chalk stream.

The infant Derwent is a tiny stream with fast, shallow runs, and small, deep, steady pools. There is an abundance of snails and small crustacea and I was not at all surprised to find that the bigger grayling were much more heavily built than those from the Wharfe, though still slimmer towards the tail than the Kennet fish. There was, nevertheless, a big surprise in store for me. The dorsal fins of some of the fish were like those from the Wharfe. But the occasional grayling here and there had a scalloped trailing edge, which in outline was just like a perch's fin.

The chalk stream we visited a few miles from Driffield is fast flowing. The grayling are plump, but not so heavily built as the Kennet fish. Here, though, there is everything in the way of dorsal fins. Mostly they are the more usual angular kind, but occasionally there are the rounded and the scalloped types.

My curiosity about grayling variations continued to

grow, even to the extent of taking time off from salmon fishing on the Tweed to catch some of the grayling there. They are fine, hard-fighting fish, a little plumper than the Wharfe grayling. Also the lower jaws are slightly shorter, and odd specimens among the smaller ones have the beak-like nose and bulge on the forward part of the belly similar to the Manifold fish.

Back home again, I felt very foolish for not having fished the Ribble. This river is much more alkaline than most of its neighbours and has a reputation for yielding heavy grayling. The omission was soon rectified and the fish I caught were of the medium-heavy build, but otherwise much like the Wharfe grayling.

As, over the years, I went further afield to sample the grayling fishing, it was the natural thing for me to make comparisons with the fish I had first known – those from the higher reaches of the fast, shallow, pebbly streams in the Yorkshire Dales. From my present, wider perspective, it seems that this type of grayling is, in fact, rather exceptional and not the norm which I originally took it to be. The shorter lower jaw seen elsewhere is certainly much more common, and it appears that the Wharfe, Yore and Swale produce the least heavily built type of grayling that is to be found. Also, I now consider that among the smaller fish specimens with the beak-like nose and bulge on the forward part of the belly are likely to occur in any water where the food is very plentiful.

It is well known that unlike trout, all grayling are naturally bred, also that water where they regenerate must be very pure and well aerated. (Trout can thrive in some kinds of slight pollution that grayling will not tolerate). These factors no doubt account, at least in part, for grayling invariably being excellent eating. And since they are entirely wild fish, it would seem that there must be some purpose in nature for the variations which occur. It is hard to imagine any advantage to the fish that might be gained by the differences in the dorsal fins. But the position of the mouth in the beak-like type could conceivably assist it in certain kinds of bottom feeding.

No doubt the variations are all part of the evolution of the fish. It would be interesting to know which of them are the more recent developments. Perhaps the scientists could answer these questions. I'm afraid I don't know whether any work has been done in this subject.

It might be expected that, since grayling vary somewhat physically in some kinds of water, there would be differences in their general habits. I do not think that this is so to any significant extent. Broadly speaking, I have found the same methods of fishing successful on every river I have fished. I was once told when fishing for rainbow trout one September on the Derbyshire Wye that the grayling there are entirely bottom feeders and ignore the dry-fly. A few minutes later I saw a dimple in mid-stream. I guessed it was neither a rainbow nor a brownie. I put my tiny, sparsely dressed Grey Duster over the spot and it was sucked under before it had travelled more than a few inches. I was quite delighted that the fish did, in fact, turn out to be a pretty little grayling.

There is a marked difference in the way trout fight in different waters and as one hears it said of some rivers that the grayling are poor fighters, it may seem reasonable to assume that they give a better performance in some places than others. Once again, I don't think there is any real difference wherever you go. Of course, chance grayling hooked in summer should be ignored. The grayling season proper does not start until the summer warmth is out of the water, which may happen during September or as late as mid October. Then the grayling get into their best condition and can be judged fairly.

It must be acknowledged that if there is not much current, some grayling can be drawn into the net before they seem to realise what is happening. Others will put up very little resistance until they see the net, and then a spirited fight commences. An occasional grayling will jump and run like a rainbow trout. In a pool where there is a good depth, some will bore down and hug the bottom, and such fish feel very heavy indeed. But the typical fight of the grayling, which is so much admired by the enthusiast, is when the fish is downstream in a strong current, and cunningly uses the hook-hold as a pivot on which to twist and turn its body, thus using the weight of the water to the maximum. This is quite a test of fine tackle and the angler's skill. And it certainly makes nonsense of suggestions that grayling are poor fighters. The type of sport they give is, indeed, quite unique – something that must be experienced to be appreciated.

After making allowances, however, for the fact that you can never say just how any individual grayling is going to fight, I think it is true to say that the overall pattern is the same quite irrespective of the river. Naturally, the more solid the current, the more confidently can one expect a good fight, and the slacker the flow, the bigger the chance that some grayling will seem lazy. But I have never seen anything to suggest that given suitable weather and water conditions, the grayling of any one river differ very much in their fighting ability from those elsewhere.

Common also to all the rivers I have fished is the frequently unpredictable way in which grayling come on to the feed and go off. You can never look out of the window in the morning and say with certainty that it is going to be a perfect grayling day. Nor can you ever safely say that you will be missing nothing if you do not go to the river.

There are, nevertheless, several extremely useful rule of thumb guides and most grayling fishers can give a fairly good forecast of the day's prospects within certain limitations. One thing that is always worth remembering is that there are very few days indeed when the grayling will not move well at some time or other. On apparently exactly similar days, good spells of extremely ready response can occur at very different times. And on the occasions when the grayling have been rather quiet for most of the day, they often take very freely indeed during the last hour of daylight.

In the early part of the grayling season before the very cold weather sets in, the availability of natural fly-food – either of aquatic or land origin – is normally the key to the problem. But frequently when some of the grayling in a pool are feeding greedily on surface flies, others can be seen lying quite dormant and cannot be tempted to show interest in any kind of artificial. Thus it can be seen that since individual fish sometimes react differently from others in the same situation, there cannot be any infallible way of anticipating in all cases how the mood of the grayling will be affected by the ruling circumstances.

Grayling fishers do not worry about this point, or even regret it. In many ways it is more interesting to have to wait and see what happens, than to know for certain in advance.

In the depths of winter when there is practically no surface activity, the problem of judging whether or not the grayling will be feeding is complicated by another, completely different factor. The fish then tend to gather in large shoals and these sometimes move considerable distances. A normally well populated pool can easily be quite devoid of fish for a period, and the first priority becomes the locating of a shoal. Only when this has been done can it be established whether or not the grayling are in a feeding humour. Many times the only way of being certain that you are actually covering fish is to catch one. Thus it is that the two sides of the question can be completely interdependent. If you catch grayling, you know both that you have found the fish and that they are feeding. If you don't catch them, you don't necessarily know whether you have failed to find the fish or if the lack of sport is because the grayling are not taking.

There are, however, so many different interesting points concerning the weather and water conditions when the grayling respond well to fly or bait or both, that it is best to deal with them in direct conjunction with the consideration of the different styles of fishing that are practised as the season progresses.

Much more remains to be discussed, then, about the behaviour of the grayling. But this I will say now. It is forty years since I caught my first grayling. Some few years later I thought my fairly regular good baskets showed that I knew the habits, likings and dislikes of the species pretty well. Since those days I have gradually learned to realise that there is no finality to the process of getting to know grayling. This ensures that grayling fishing can never become stale, and for that I am indeed grateful.

Dry-fly Considerations

At the end of his first season of dry-fly fishing for trout, the novice is very alive to the difficulty of approaching a rising fish without scaring it. He will confess that often he was unable to test his skill in placing the artificial effectively: the trout had departed before he was within casting distance.

It comes as a very pleasant surprise to him to discover that the grayling is much more tolerant of the figure of the angler on the bank. Fast movements and casting shadows over the fish should be avoided, but creeping and crawling are quite unnecessary. At some times the grayling may seem a little more sensitive than at others, but normally one can move forward in full view of the fish to a suitable casting position without upsetting them at all.

When the light is favourable, it is quite delightful to be able to stand and watch a grayling rise from the bottom and approach the artificial. It may take solidly the first time, or perform a variety of tricks. Sometimes it will mouth the fly tentatively without getting a proper hold. Alternatively it will nudge the fly, splash at it, or turn away at the last moment without actually touching it.

Whatever the nature of a grayling's frolicking with the fly, however, it will probably come again at the next cast, and try something different. Another common variation is for the fish to let the fly travel a yard or two downstream of its lie, as if ignoring it entirely; then turn, swim calmly after it, and take with a lovely bulge.

Certainly it is a frequent occurrence for a grayling to make numerous approaches to the fly before it is finally hooked, and one should never despair of catching a fish that seems to want only to play with the fly. The chances are that ultimately it will rise purposefully and take with supreme confidence.

This is a peculiarity of dry-fly fishing for grayling and rarely, if ever, occurs with wet-fly. Of course, there are many days when the fish will take the dry-fly seriously at the first attempt and other occasions when they do not come a second time if they fail the first. But normally the novice will find the grayling willing to give him plenty of practice at striking. He will probably get more experience of testing his reactions to offers from fish in one hour when the grayling are in an interested mood than he will in days of dry-fly fishing for trout.

One common experience with grayling really does highlight how much more accommodating they are than trout. After a fish has been hooked in mid-stream at the fourth or fifth cast, another grayling will often rise closer to the bank in the area that has been traversed by the line several times. One would think that such a fish would be in no mood to give any consideration to the artificial. Not at all – it is just as likely to be caught as any other fish. It is interesting to speculate why this is so. Even when a grayling is rising regularly at short intervals (not smutting) it returns to its lie on the bottom every time, no matter how deep the water. It seems that the line floating on the surface above the fish is accepted as a harmless event and not at all worrying. When eventually the artificial covers the lie, the impact is quite unimpaired and the grayling responds to the urge of its hunger or curiosity.

Tackle presents no difficult problem. Any modern,

light fly rod of about 8 foot 6 inches with a quick action is suitable.

The lightest line that will give reasonable command of the water is to be preferred to an unnecessarily heavy one. Usually there will be no serious difficulty concerning wind, because dry-fly fishing is essentially a method for reasonably calm weather or well sheltered parts of the river. Consequently an AFTM # 6 (old No. 3) is as heavy as most people will ever require, while a # 5 (old No. 2) is to be favoured if it will give adequate coverage of the pools.

Some little care is required in selecting the nylon for the casts because a fine point, no stronger than three lb, is desirable. In some brands, this strength will land fish after fish without any breakages. In others, the fine nylon soon starts to 'neck' at the point where the fly is attached. This weakens it tremendously and eventually it breaks on a fish when no undue pressure is being used. Also to be avoided is any make of nylon that becomes curled close to where the fly has been tied on. It will be found that the brands that can be knotted without curling are also free from the troublesome 'necking'. It does pay, therefore, to do a little experimenting before deciding which kind of nylon to buy.

The flies required include a few popular trout patterns, and a small variety of the traditional grayling flies. This is very much a matter of personal preference and confidence, and the individual is sure to develop ideas of his own, even if he is willing to accept advice at the beginning. Therefore, the first need here is to consider the minimum basic requirements, which can be added to later as desired.

The trout patterns most likely to be wanted are those covering the duns of the pale watery, medium olive, iron blue, and blue winged olive, and also the black gnat. Any popular dressings are quite suitable. All should be lightly dressed and it is unlikely that anything bigger than a No. 16 will be needed, while smaller sizes are often preferable. At the same time, on some of the chalkstreams, such as the Test and the Itchen, where the flow is very strong and grayling in excess of two lb are not uncommon, 14s and even 12s are often used. This, however, is done more with a view to playing the fish on a bigger, stronger hook, than to suggest that a larger artificial is required to attract the grayling.

Dark needle flies are often plentiful; but although as a wet-fly this species is very popular, it is rare that imitations of the mature fly are used for dry-fly fishing.

In selecting the fancy grayling flies, the main objective should be to get an adequate coverage of the different basic colours, and at the same time to make sure that patterns are included which are easy to see on the water whatever the state of the light and the background. Red Tag, Sturdy's Fancy or Rolt's Witch, Grayling Steel Blue, Yellow Bumble, and Green Insect should fill all requirements to start with. Once again, the flies should be lightly dressed on 16s and smaller.

Some anglers believe that certain grayling patterns have a particular and decided charm for the fish. There is no doubt that there are days when a darkish fly does best and other times when the fish show a preference for a paler coloured pattern. But in my opinion, no one pattern in any particular colour range has any great advantage over the others of similar tone. I think it is more important to use a fly that can be seen well by the angler and floats high on the water, than to sacrifice either of those two features in favour of another pattern purely on the grounds that it enjoys a specially good reputation. As dry-flies, the bumbles owe much of their success to the excellent way they float, while Sturdy's Fancy, which accounts for a great number of grayling, is extremely useful because the cream hackle can be seen against a dark background, and the peacock herl body and the tag of red silk or wool show up well on bright patches of water.

Every grayling fisher is sure to say that the flies mentioned ought most definitely to include some other pattern. For instance the Treacle Parkin is a very popular fly, is easy to see in most lights, floats well, and is taken freely by the grayling everywhere. But surely the insistence by one angler that his favourite fly is best and by others that different patterns again are too deadly to be ignored, must prove the point that the precise dressing of the fly is not terribly important as far as the grayling are concerned.

The fly floatant is a vital item in dry-fly fishing for grayling. I melt a touch of solid line grease on my finger tip and stroke this on to the hackle and body. Even on very damp autumn days, it is very effective. It may be found after a few fish have been taken on the one fly that it is necessary to dry it and apply more grease, but after a minute of this treatment it rides high on the water again.

Phases of Dry-fly Fishing

Good sport with dry-fly for grayling can be roughly
divided into four different categories. Firstly there is the
situation in late September or October when a hatch of
duns takes place during the middle of the day. The trout
will be feeding on the nymph, or the hatching dun, in the
streamier water. Usually the grayling will avoid being in
too close proximity with the trout, and will wait for the
floating duns to reach them in the smoother water further
down the pool, or in the glide at the tail of the pool.

The shoal of grayling would probably have been
located, owing to its being seen smutting, well in
advance of the start of the hatch. Possibly, too, they
would have ignored any artificial offered to them
although it was surrounded all the time by the dimples
of the smutting fish.

Perhaps the first few duns to sail down will go by
unmolested, but soon one grayling will start sampling
the flies and before long many of them will settle down
to steady feeding.

The choice of the artificial to represent the natural fly
on the water is much less exacting than it sometimes
is with the trout. It is quite safe to say that so long as
the shade is roughly right and the fly floats high on
the water, the details of the dressing are not important.
Interchanging standard trout patterns and fancy grayling
flies of a similar shade does not seem to make any
difference, and thus one is free to give preference

to whichever dressing floats the best. Also one can pander to personal fancies. I am inclined to favour the Grey Duster for the pale watery and the lighter coloured medium olives; the John Storey for the darker olives; and the Grayling Steel Blue for the iron blue dun and the blue winged olive dun. This small mixture of flies may be thought to be an oversimplification of the problem, but the novice can be assured that it will be very adequate until such a time as he begins to pursue his personal line of thought on the subject.

In these circumstances it is very effective to fish very much as one would do for trout, even to the extent of allowing the fish to take the fly down beneath the surface before tightening. I favour fishing as squarely as possible, or drifting the fly downstream if this can be done without much drag, but if the situation will only permit upstream fishing, it will usually be quite effective during these periods when the grayling are feeding on duns. If, however, a fish proves stubborn, the answer is nearly certain to be that the fly must lead the cast as it covers the fish. This is easy to do from any position if the air current is downstream. In the absence of such help, it may be necessary to restrict oneself to square casts and making upstream mends so that the fly goes first over the fish.

The mending technique is not difficult. The fly is cast about three yards upstream of the grayling, and about the same distance beyond the intended line of drift of the fly. The line is then lobbed over in the upstream direction and this draws the fly into the correct position to float over the fish. Fly, cast and line are then allowed to drift freely.

Mending brings another, incidental, benefit. Frequently, when the fly first lights on the surface it settles in the skin of the water instead of standing high on the hackle. The way the fly is drawn across the water during the mend pulls it up on to the hackle points and makes it ride exactly as is wanted. Even when mending is unnecessary, it is good policy to give the line a little twitch as soon as the fly has settled so that it will float correctly.

The novice will regard drag as an unforgivable sin in all circumstances. He will remember how, at the last moment when a trout was going to take his fly, the slightest bit of drag developed, and the fish immediately turned away. He will quickly find that he can take a much more light-hearted view of drag when grayling fishing.

If the fish are feeding steadily and seriously on the floating dun, it is an advantage to avoid drag so that the artificial will travel directly down over a grayling, thus giving it the easiest opportunity to take. But very often in these circumstances, the fly is taken by another fish lower down after it has started to drag quite perceptibly. The most important feature of drag, though, is that if the grayling do not seem to be very hungry and are letting a lot of the naturals go by, periodic twitches on the line that cause little spells of drag seem to focus attention onto the artificial and induce a good, solid take.

The frequent advantage of employing drag is one reason why so many grayling fishers recommend that one should always fish the dry-fly downstream. In this way, the line is nearly always tight enough to strike effectively when the rise comes. When fishing a longish line upstream, there is usually some unavoidable slack line by the time the fly has started to drag attractively, and then the effect of the strike can be delayed too long to hook the fish.

The interest of the grayling in a hatch of duns is not restricted to clear water conditions. Some of the best sport with dry-fly is to be had on a nice sunny day when the river is still coloured after a spate. Deep water, of course, should be avoided. A steady glide of between one and two feet in depth is likely to be the best, but one should be guided first and foremost by the surface activity of the fish. If the water is really high, it may be that most of the grayling rises will be within inches of the bank. It is then the best policy to work steadily up a short stretch, not spending too much time on any one fish that is not very obliging. Soon the same stretch can be fished up again and this time the previously awkward ones will probably take, while rises will appear again at the points where fish were hooked the first time up. Some fine catches are made on dry-fly in this way, and in my opinion, this is much preferable to resorting to wet-fly, although, of course, that too would probably be quite effective as an alternative.

The next category of dry-fly fishing is when there is no specific hatch of any one kind of dun, and the grayling are taking a variety of both aquatic flies and ones blown from the trees or the land. Often in October on a breezy day when there are gusts of strong wind, good grayling will be seen to be feeding well in the calmer areas below overhanging trees. They take practically everything that comes their way from large autumn duns down to tiny little shiny black flies that come from the trees.

Some anglers have favourite patterns for these conditions, a black gnat being very popular, but almost any fly in the box is well worth trying if one's first choice does not seem very successful. A Sturdy's Fancy on a No. 18 is a good fly to start with. When this has taken two or three grayling and the others within reach have all had a good look at it, a Grayling Steel Blue may kill one or two more. This, in turn, will probably seem to go stale, and then it is a good plan to try the Sturdy's Fancy again.

Changes in the light should be noted carefully. Normally in this kind of situation there will be intermittent spells of sunshine. It may be found that one pattern kills best in the strong light and another when the sun is clouded over. And if either strength of light seems to make the fish less keen, a change to the other should be the cue to start casting again.

It is when the grayling are feeding on a very mixed variety of natural flies that they are most likely to make several approaches to the artificial before finally taking properly. Sometimes if there are several fish rising within casting distance from the one stand – as often there will be – it pays to cast once to each in turn, catch all the most willing ones quickly, and then move on and repeat the performance in the next good place.

On the other hand, it may be found that none of the fish take solidly at the first cast, but a few are hooked after being offered the fly several times. In such cases, it seems that the grayling's confidence that the artificial is something that they really ought to feed on has to be built up by numerous repeated sightings of the same item. In this respect grayling fishers have often said jokingly that they had to create a 'hatch' of Treacle Parkins before the fish would take, or that they had to do some 'groundbaiting' with the Red Tag to get the grayling into the right mood. However, when the fish do require this coaxing it is the best policy to concentrate on each individual fish until either it is caught or it becomes obvious that too much time is being wasted. But any stubborn fish should be tried again soon afterwards, because a short interval often makes all the difference and the grayling then takes readily.

It will usually be found that the spots most favoured by the grayling in this context get the full benefit of any sunshine there might be. Areas permanently shaded at that particular time of the day are unlikely to be very productive. A nice flow of water to carry the flies on the surface over the fish is also necessary to provide the most favourable prospects. A few grayling may swim round a patch of dead water and gather up any water-logged insects, but it requires the steady arrival of items of tasty fly food to hold a shoal of good fish in a confined space and keep them in an active mood.

Familiarity with a stretch of river makes it possible in these conditions to anticipate which will be the best places according to the direction of the wind and thus save valuable time. It is very gratifying, after a quick glance at the water, to make a bee-line to a favourite, cosy corner and find that, sure enough, the grayling are feeding on the surface, while elsewhere the river is generally wind-swept and uninviting.

When there is a blustery, downstream wind, one such sheltered cast on the Wharfe is from beneath a public footpath running beside the river and several feet above water level. On numerous occasions several passers-by have gathered there in full view of the fish to watch the grayling rising to my dry-fly and this has not interfered with sport at all. There is no doubt that when grayling are feeding keenly on the surface, they are very single-minded and are not easily upset by happenings outside their own immediate environment.

The gusts of wind that bring the insects from the trees and banks also cause dead leaves to fall and sometimes the water is carpeted with them. But this is no detriment to sport. The grayling obviously know all about the excellent prospects of food appearing in these circumstances and the leaves seem to make them more watchful. Certainly they will not fail to spot the dry-fly, although the angler may find it more difficult to keep his eye on it than when it is floating on a clear surface.

A very pleasing feature of this kind of situation is that it seems to arouse the interest of all sizes of grayling, including the larger ones. There are some occasions when sport with the dry-fly is confined to the medium sized and smaller fish, but this never seems to be the case when windy weather produces a mixed feast in a sheltered corner.

Incidentally, when the fly gets caught up on a floating leaf, do not try to dislodge it by false casting. Leaves tend to spin like propellers and put an enormous amount of twist and kink into the fine nylon. In no time it can be so bad that the cast is in a hopeless state and has to be discarded.

The third category of dry-fly fishing can be a little unreliable, but when it is good, it is most enjoyable and can produce some fine baskets. It occurs when the grayling are engaged in very industrious smutting, and natural flies of any appreciable size are very scarce.

On odd occasions of that kind the grayling will ignore all efforts with any kind of artificial. Usually, however, they cannot resist for very long a small fly floating high on the water, and as soon as one offer comes, more can be expected to follow with fair certainty.

In these circumstances, the grayling play all sorts of pranks with the fly and it is usually the best policy to strike instantly at every touch of any sort. Many of the strikes will be unavailing, but often when it seems impossible that the fish could have got the fly into its mouth in the time, it will be found to be solidly hooked in the upper lip. If the strike is delayed, the fly will be seen to continue floating along as if nothing had touched it.

This kind of dry-fly fishing has induced some anglers to try very small double hooks in the hope of hooking a better percentage of the grayling. I do not like this idea. It makes it more difficult to keep the fly floating high enough, and I think it increases the risk that the fly will not enter the grayling's mouth properly when the extremely rapid and minute suck of the fish is made.

Often the offers of the fish make only the tiniest of dimples and it is hard to believe that anything has happened that is worth striking at. Yet it will sometimes be found that these almost imperceptible offers result in hooking some of the biggest grayling. It is worth repeating that the quickest possible strike should be made at any indication of interference with the fly.

Smutting by the grayling is restricted to reasonably calm weather. The most favourable conditions are when some patches in an area of smooth water are untouched by the breeze, but other parts are very slightly rippled. The dimples will be confined to the unrippled surface, and some grayling will come to the artificial there, but the deadliest spot is just on the edge of the ripple. The imparting of periodic touches of drag to the fly usually proves very attractive: indeed, there are occasions when this is essential to success.

It is usually best to use the smallest size of flies, but I have never found any extra benefit in attempting to copy any sort of natural smut on a minute hook. Such experiments have certainly accounted for the odd grayling or two, but I have satisfied myself that it is not a worthwhile proposition.

Many grayling fishers stick to a small black gnat when the fish are smutting. This can be quite successful, but I do not think the grayling take it for an overgrown version of the natural smut and I consider that it has no pull in that direction. Certainly many other flies – in fact almost any pattern – will do equally well at times, and therefore it is reasonable to argue that the best policy is to use a pattern that can be seen well – and can be seen to be floating well.

I must confess, though, that if my early efforts are not successful, I am tempted to change my fly before long. But I am sure that it is the time factor that is important, not the pattern of the fly, because on many occasions when the fish have eventually started to show interest in a fresh fly, I have reverted to one of those that were previously refused, and the offers have kept on coming just the same.

The most hectic sport with this class of fishing is often towards dusk. It is probable, too, that if only the medium sized and smaller fish were interested earlier on, the larger ones will start feeding when the light begins to fade. And the nearer it gets to darkness, the keener the grayling become. Then it is best to fish a very short line, and very shallow water at the edge of the river will often yield the heavier specimens.

This sometimes reveals one of the many puzzling peculiarities in the habits of the grayling. Once good sport has been had at dusk in a particular shallow area close in at the side of the river, it is always worth trying there again on future occasions. I have no very firm idea as to why the grayling favour some such areas and ignore others which appear to be exactly similar. But the regularity with which this happens suggests that there must be some very good, material reason for it.

By the time of the year when evening fly fishers on northern streams have switched their attention from the trout to the grayling, sedges and moths have ceased to be at all plentiful, and small artificials are used almost exclusively. But on chalkstreams in the south, I am told, big bushily dressed sedges and moths will sometimes take grayling when they do not appear to have any interest in small dry flies.

The fourth and final category of dry-fly fishing is in a class quite on its own and can provide a unique kind of satisfaction.

On a calm day with a clear sky following a frosty night in late autumn or early winter, when there are virtually no natural flies on the water, occasional rises are seen here and there. Other grayling can be seen lying on the gravel at the bottom where the water is not too deep.

In these conditions, the Sturdy's Fancy, Grayling Steel Blue or whatever fly is fancied most, can be seen floating down as clearly as if it were a top hat, and even the fine nylon at the point of the cast looks like a hawser on the smooth surface. Yet the grayling – no doubt feeling the pangs of hunger – will take the fly with beautiful rises that send rings spreading for yards across the water. Now a slightly larger fly – a No. 14 – may perhaps be taken quite freely. In that case some anglers consider it an advantage to use the bigger hook, believing that it improves the chance of getting a secure hold. But any failure to get serious rises from the grayling should be seen as a cue that a smaller fly is needed.

When a grayling has been spotted – whether or not it has been seen to rise – it will often take the fly greedily at the first offering. Other grayling may have a preliminary look at the fly before attempting to take it, but when the real rise comes, it is usually a solid take.

Particularly from the visual point of view, this is exceptionally entertaining sport. Suitable days are not very common, but when they do come, they are most memorable.

An interesting coincidence occurred one such lovely November day some years ago. Jack Aykroyd, Gerald Dyson and I were strolling up the Wharfe, they with trotting outfits and I with a fly rod. We had been discussing some diagrams in a popular new fishing book which showed grayling rising to the dry-fly. The author claimed that they only ever took directly above their lies or lower downstream, and never rose to intercept the fly ahead of their position on the bottom.

Soon I spotted a grayling lying a few yards from the bank in about eighteen inches of water and suggested that Jack should show it the gilt-tail. Several times the worm drifted down near the grayling, so close on one or two occasions that the fish moved aside to let it go past. It became quite clear that the grayling had not the slightest interest in the gilt-tail. I then dropped my Grayling Steel Blue a couple of yards upstream of the fish, while, incidentally, all three of us were standing in full view of the fish. As the fly approached, the grayling lifted and went forward a few inches, but then dropped back to its lie. The next time down, it set off at about 45° up towards the fly and got about half way to it when, as before, it dropped back to the bottom. On the third cast, the grayling came right up to the fly a full yard ahead of its lie, but did not touch it and again returned to its lie. The fourth appearance of the fly again brought the grayling right up to it in about the same position as the previous time. For a moment the grayling dropped down with the current and with its nose practically touching the fly. Then, very slowly and casually it seemed, the fish took. I tightened instantly. The grayling – about ¾lb – was hooked well inside the top jaw.

It may be that in deeper water grayling do not take the dry-fly upstream of their lies, but it is certainly not so in reasonably shallow water. Of course, the value of this study is the guide it gives in the matter of how far ahead of the fish the fly ought to be placed. It is certainly advisable to have the fly drift over the fish from a point as high upstream of the lie as is practicable – as much as two or three yards. This does not matter so much when the grayling are taking very greedily, but it can make the difference between success and failure when some coaxing is necessary.

As the season advances, suitable days for dry-fly fishing become scarcer, but even in the depths of winter, the grayling will come to the surface for the fly when conditions are favourable. Once during the Christmas Holidays, however, I saw Harry Wood, the well-known Bolton Abbey fly-fisher, taking grayling on the dry-fly although the sky was leaden and the atmosphere very raw indeed. He was fishing a short line upstream in smooth, very shallow water, where few anglers would have thought any grayling would be lying.

Unless conditions are very promising for the dry-fly during December onwards, I resort to the wet-fly or trotting the gilt-tail. It is too much of a gamble to go to the river unprepared for these alternatives. But equally it is a mistake ever to fail to have dry-fly tackle available, because an unexpected change in the weather often brings ideal conditions for a few hours.

One December day some ten or twelve years ago, I had a novel experience with the dry-fly. Following a night frost, there was a cloudless sky and the air was dead still. As soon as I reached the river, I saw a rise and my Grayling Steel Blue was accepted immediately.

On landing the fish I saw another rise a short distance upstream. That grayling was just as obliging as the first one, and having dealt with it, I again saw the rings of a rise spreading across the river a little higher up. Thus it went on: on each occasion when I had landed a fish, I had little or no time to wait before another one was tempting me further upstream. Eventually when the light began to go I was quite a way up the river and had two difficult stretches of bank to negotiate on my return journey. There was no moon, and before I had gone far, it was very dark indeed despite the absence of cloud. As I picked my way along the riverside, I heard the plop of a fish, which seemed to come from about mid-stream. Thoughts of night fishing in summer for sea trout sprang to my mind. I started casting, more, I must acknowledge, because I simply could not resist than in the hope of anything happening. However, after about the third throw, there was another plop that sounded to be in about the right place. I tightened, the strain of a fish was there, and after a splendid fight I was elated to see that the fish in the net was indeed a good grayling. On two further occasions on the way downstream the same thing happened. Three grayling taken in the darkness on dry-fly was proof enough to say that there was nothing freakish about it. A perfect day in winter is apparently too short for the grayling, just as it is for the angler.

More recently, Oliver Kite told me about catching grayling in the dark on nymph and he has covered this subject most interestingly in his book 'Nymph Fishing in Practice' (published by Herbert Jenkins).

There is no doubt that when the grayling are taking at the close of day, the darkness does not put an end to their interest.

A favourable feature of all dry-fly fishing is that very few grayling are lost during the fight, although they are generally considered to be very soft mouthed. When a fish takes a fly on the surface, it is nearly always hooked in the top jaw. This gives a very secure hold: indeed, it is often impossible to get the hook out without breaking off the barb. This is a hazard which must be watched carefully. The sides of the mouth, however, are very tender and the hook tears away very easily.

Many fly-fishers in the North habitually use wet-fly because they have the notion that dry-fly is too difficult and they lack confidence in themselves. I have no hesitation in saying that it is much more difficult to fish well with wet-fly than with dry-fly. If an angler is reasonably successful with wet-fly he will find that on suitable days, dry-fly will present him with no difficulty that he will not manage to overcome relatively easily.

I think the idea that dry-fly fishing is difficult must date back to the times of the problems associated with the use of silkworm gut casts. With correctly balanced modern tackle and good, fine, nylon points, every angler should soon be able to fish the dry-fly for grayling well enough to have a thoroughly enjoyable time.

Some Wet-fly Problems

Even the most experienced anglers with wet-fly for grayling will acknowledge that they usually get a lot of plucks that come to nothing and that they lose quite a few of the fish they hook. Splendid catches on wet-fly are nevertheless commonplace, but seldom is there not some feeling that one might have made more of the opportunities that came.

This may seem rather a questionable recommendation for the wet-fly method, but I think it ought to be said so that the novice will not get too poor an opinion of his performance during his early efforts. He can be assured that careful attention to a few details will quickly bring results that are good enough to make his fishing very absorbing.

Perhaps the best way to show how the flies are best fished is to stress first the principal causes of failure. If a cast is made at 45° downstream and the flies are allowed to drift round on a tight line, the grayling will most probably come and snatch at them, but very few fish indeed will be hooked properly. By the time the offer has been felt through the rod, the grayling has had the chance to feel the resistance of the tackle, and will nearly always be quicker in ejecting the fly than the angler will be in striking. It follows that before the fish realises too acutely that it has made a mistake, the angler wants all the warning of an offer he can get so that he can tighten while the fly is still in the grayling's mouth.

The easiest way to achieve this is to cast almost square, or perhaps slightly upstream, and hold the rod fairly high so that the line curves steeply to the water. The rod point should follow, always pointing to the flies, as the line drifts round. The end of the line and the area covered by the flies must be watched carefully. A floating line should be used.

A fish may be seen to come and take; there may be a swirl near the surface; or alternatively the end of the line will suddenly move forward. But whichever one of these indications of an offer is detected, the strike can be made before anything is felt in the rod hand, and will normally be in time to hook the grayling.

An awkward breeze or an unfavourable set of the current can make it difficult to fish the cast round entirely satisfactorily, and then it is not easy to avoid being too slow to hook some of the grayling that rise. But lowering the rod point in the hope of reducing the delay before a strike is effective is no remedy. This also reduces the delay before the fish feels the resistance of the tackle, and increases the risk that a worthless pluck will be felt before any visual warning of the offer is seen.

It will be appreciated that there is a very decided top limit to the length of line that will allow the best use of this method. If too much line is out, one is nearly certain to be back in the position where the pluck is felt before anything is seen. Therefore, the soundest policy is to fish the shortest line that will cover the lies adequately, and never resort to lengthening of the line where a change of the casting position will do instead.

Another important point in this connection is that the flies should not be dropped beyond the line of the fastest flow of the current. If that is done, the pull of the line drags the flies round too quickly until they reach the fastest current. Then they may fish correctly but no better than they would do after a subsequent cast with the shorter line from a point a few paces downstream. Consequently, the longer line achieves nothing and reduces the chance of hooking some fish that should not otherwise be difficult to catch.

The most helpful type of flow is where the speed reduces evenly between the point where the flies fall and the position of the rod. There the cast fishes round beautifully and the best possible chance is given to tighten on a fish quickly enough and get a firm hook-hold.

If the fastest current is divided into two or more branches, it usually pays to make the most of the nearest one and ignore the others. Certainly offers will probably be got if a longer line is fished to reach beyond the first line of faster water, but most of them will be the useless kind of plucks. And once again, the longer line swinging round spoils the prospects of the water closer to the bank being fished to the best advantage.

Now it will be seen that for wet-fly fishing, it is helpful to have a longer rod than for dry-fly. I have no complaint against the modern cult of short rods for dry-fly. Unfortunately, though, this seems to have created a popular demand that every rod should have the maximum casting power for its length. Manufacturers cannot afford to ignore this, with the result that today it is difficult to find a first class wet-fly rod. What is wanted primarily is good reach with lightness and quick action. Potential in the way of throwing a great length of line is quite irrelevant. I have a three piece, eleven foot rod that had to be specially made. A big sea trout would probably ruin it, but for wet-fly for grayling, and for brown trout, it is delightful. It fishes an AFTM # 5 (old No. 2) line nicely and is not the least bit tiring. Furthermore, a back-cast is seldom necessary. A little lift of the rod and a gentle switch puts the line out again perfectly, thus saving time and the possible risk of getting hung up behind.

It may be thought that it is too costly in time always to avoid the long line that will apparently give coverage of the water more quickly. But when a shoal of interested grayling has been found, the objective is to catch the maximum number of fish in the shortest length of time and the least area of water possible. The short line is undoubtedly the way to achieve this. Each cast should cover a new drift, because the first sight of the flies by the fish is the most effective – possibly the only effective one at that particular time. The artificial beneath the surface does not retain its power of deception anything like the dry-fly, which has to be viewed by the grayling through the skin of the water that is distorted by the hackle points. Therefore it is seldom worthwhile to cast more than once in exactly the same place, and it is best to move down the pool at least a yard at a time. However, when a point is reached where offers are getting scarce and it is suspected that one is beyond the bottom limit of the shoal, enough time will have elapsed for the fish to be sufficiently rested for the pool to be fished down again. Often the second or third time down the pool will produce as many fish as the first. Grayling seem to have a much shorter memory than trout. A fish that was risen and missed as little as ten minutes earlier is likely to come again for the fly quite boldly.

The old, traditional idea that you should always fish downstream for grayling is no more true of wet-fly than it is of dry-fly. Dr Ian Calvert-Wilson, who has no peer as a fly-fisherman for trout on the rivers of the North, fishes up and across almost invariably. He contends – and I do not dispute his view - that many more of the grayling that rise are hooked securely than when the fish are downstream of the angler. I rarely settle down to planned upstream fishing with wet-fly because when the weather is calm enough to make this attractive, I much prefer dry-fly. However, with the wet-fly I do occasionally cast up and across, but for a different purpose. It is to allow the flies to sink much deeper as they drift down, and when the line is a little below me, I check so that the flies rise towards the surface. This is often a very effective manoeuvre when the fish do not seem very keen on the flies moving round at a more constant level. Of course, fishing in Ian's style results in this lift to the flies to a minor degree every time the cast is withdrawn from the water for another throw. Quite often a grayling takes at the last moment, practically on the surface.

Ian's inseparable companion on his weekly trips to the Yore throughout the grayling season is Len Stott, of salmon fishing fame. Len does not follow the policy of his friend. He fishes across and down, is a great believer in working the flies, and seldom allows them to drift naturally for long. Inching the line in with the left hand, or periodically lifting the rod tip, certainly does make the flies behave more enticingly on occasions, but the novice should not work the flies as matter of course. Indeed, I hope to show that he will more often do better if he avoids giving the flies extra 'life'.

Early in the season when there is still a lot of activity in the way of flies hatching, I believe that the trout patterns which I then favour move more naturally if one simply attempts to make them drift with the current. While the cast is being fished out, the artificials automatically move across the current several yards at the same time as they travel down with it. This is obviously not accomplished as a smooth swing, but occurs in a series of short periods of acceleration and deceleration according to the way the current holds the fly here and loses its grip on it there. This is further assisted by the way the three flies on the cast work with or against each other. These changes of speed cause the hackles to flex as is intended, and altogether, as results show, the grayling are adequately deceived by this method.

In the colder months when there is little fly life to attract the attention of the fish to the surface, and fancy grayling patterns are the most effective, I think that there is a better case for working the flies. Even then, if the grayling respond satisfactorily when the flies are being fished round unchecked, it is best to refrain from giving them any added movement because this reduces the chance of hooking the fish securely.

Len Stott cheerfully argues that it is better to land sixteen grayling and miss twenty or more other plucks, than to miss fewer offers, but also make a smaller catch. As far as he personally is concerned, that is a very sound view, but he is an extremely good fisherman. The less experienced angler is likely to hook the fish solidly and finish up with a better basket if he does not attempt to work the flies. Of course, that will mean that he will not be able to catch fish in all the places where Len would succeed. However, grayling days are short, and few anglers can afford the time to fish parts of the pools other than those where the conditions favour them the most.

Before considering the actual patterns of flies to be used, it is worth giving a little thought to the mechanics, so to speak, of the wet-fly cast of three artificials. It will be appreciated that as they work down and across the current, they move at different speeds and levels.

The point fly sinks the deepest, moves the fastest and with the most variety, and towards the end of the drift, lifts through the water more than the other two. Such action is the nearest to the behaviour of some of the nymphs. The point fly position, therefore, should be reserved for the spider patterns that represent nymphs when hatching.

The bob fly (or top dropper), moves the slowest,

nearest the surface, and the most evenly. Thus it is the best position for the imitations of the dun, the drowned dun or spinner, gnats or artificials that may be taken as land flies.

The dropper, falling half way between the other two, can be used reasonably well as a duplication for either purpose if the point fly or the bob fly shows itself to be particularly attractive in the immediate conditions.

From this small study, it will be seen that the three flies should not be close together at the bottom of the cast. I like my bob fly to be no more than eighteen inches from the top of the cast, and the dropper to be equidistant between the bob and the point. It need hardly be said, of course, that where there is any risk of a dropper getting caught in weeds when a grayling is being played, it is wisest to fish a single fly only. And, by the way, always remember to treat the cast with a paste made from fuller's-earth and water to remove any tendency for it to skim on the surface.

Phases of Wet-fly and Nymph Fishing

My favourite cast for a clear water in autumn when conditions are favourable for hatches of fly is Orange Partridge and Gold Tinsel at the point, Dark Needle Fly as dropper, and according to the circumstances, Black Gnat or alternatively, Snipe and Purple for the bob fly.

It is quite remarkable that the Waterhen Bloa, which is such a superb fly in spring for trout when medium olives are hatching, does not seem to appeal very much to the grayling, although they take the natural dun of the medium olive very greedily. On several occasions I have fished two Waterhen Bloas and an Orange Partridge and Gold Tinsel, and the latter has accounted for nearly all the grayling caught, quite irrespective of its position on the cast. It can be assumed, of course, that the Orange Partridge is also taken as an immature stone fly of some sort, and there is really no proof that it ever simulates any stage of the medium olive. Nevertheless, it has more than earned its position as my standard point fly.

The Dark Needle Fly regularly justifies its use, as does the Black Gnat, but I should say the performance of the Snipe and Purple when there are some iron blue duns on the water is as good, if not better, than that of any other fly at any time. Furthermore, the bigger grayling seem to be very keen on the Snipe and Purple.

The popply, streamy water a little way below the necks of pools is much the easiest to fish well with wet-fly and also provides the most concentrated supply of hatching duns for the fish. These big attractions make it difficult for some anglers to believe that those are not the right places to fish for grayling. The reason for this is that the grayling are very timid of the trout and quite definitely have to take second place when feeding on fly. Before the hatch begins, the trout wait quietly in secluded lies and then the odd few grayling may be picked up in the streamy water. As soon as the nymphs start moving in readiness for the hatch, however, the trout lose no time in taking up their feeding positions and any grayling that were foraging there make a rapid departure.

On the chalk streams where the summer and autumn provide an over-plentiful supply of fly food for all the fish of both species, the trout are often relatively lazy and non-belligerent creatures. There grayling are commonly to be seen lying at no great distance from the trout. It is a very different matter on the rain-fed rivers. Hatches of fly can be quite lush, but usually they are well spaced and short-lived. After the long, lifeless periods of waiting, competition for the food when it finally comes is much keener. The trout are very aggressive, and if any are being caught, the angler can be certain that he will be able to find better places to fish – parts of the pools where the grayling will be feeding peacefully, free from any threat from the fearsome trout.

After about the middle of November when hatches of fly are rare and the trout are more interested in prospecting in the spawning becks, a shoal of grayling may sometimes be found near the neck of a pool: then wet-fly fishing with fancy grayling patterns can be very good indeed. But so long as good hatches of fly are the dominant factor, the glides towards the tails of pools are the most reliable places. Smooth water with a good flow

in the middle of the pool can be very good, particularly
so if the set of the current or a little breeze takes most
of the flies under overhanging branches close to a high
bank. There the biggest of the grayling are likely to be
found feeding.

Some people imagine that grayling have a preference
for sluggish water. This is quite wrong. It is true that
at times in winter the grayling like deepish water and
sometimes they will forage through the slacks. But the
water they favour the most, either when feeding on fly
or lying dormant, is where there is a good, even flow:
hence the importance of glides.

In a coloured water in the autumn, especially when
most of the rises to naturals are very close to the banks,
I prefer very meaty looking flies. A good reliable cast
is Greenwell's Glory at the point, followed by Treacle
Parkin and Bradshaw's Fancy.

In such conditions it may be that one can do no
more than bring the flies round and over the fish at
the dangle. The drag can become excessive, causing
the flies to skim rather ridiculously, but that does not
always deter the fish. There is no doubt that when the
grayling are feeding on fly in a coloured water, they
are very greedy indeed and this makes them careless.

Eventually the weather gets too cold for anything
more than a negligible amount of natural fly food for
the grayling. Then the colourfulness of the fancy grayling
patterns makes its great impact. Many anglers believe
that red is of outstanding importance. There seems
to be much justification for this view and certainly a
good number of the most famous of the grayling flies
have a tag of red silk or wool. But I try to remain
open-minded about colour, because blue and yellow
can each be so attractive at times that undoubtedly it
would be very wrong always to ignore them in favour
of red. However, I usually take the easy way out of the

situation by including flies on my cast featuring all three of those colours. My favourite trio is Red Tag at the point, Yellow Bumble on the dropper and Grayling Steel Blue as the bob fly. I must say immediately, though, that when the grayling are moving well to the wet-fly in late autumn and winter, I do not think any of the well known patterns would ever fail to give a good account of themselves.

If the weather is fairly open and the water being fished not generally deeper than about three feet, normally dressed flies are suitable. And the fishing tactics employed with wet-fly earlier in the season when duns were hatching continue to be the most effective. Also the same sizes of hook – 16s and smaller – are still to be preferred.

When conditions become less favourable – colder, duller or more windy – or if the river is rather bolder and the current stronger, it is often better to use leaded flies of the same patterns. Some anglers then prefer slightly bigger hooks – 14s – but I am still quite happy with 16s.

The chief problem with leaded flies is to ascertain the depth at which they attract the grayling the most readily. If they are fished across and down in the usual way, and with the line still floating, they will not go deeper than about a foot in a reasonably steady flow, and that often proves to be about right for good response. However, if the flies are placed slightly upstream, they will go deeper, and the point fly may reach a depth of about two feet. Of course, if the Red Tag on the point is then taken at two feet down, or the Grayling Steel Blue on the bob at only about one foot, it may be that it is the pattern and not the depth that is responsible. However, a little more exploratory fishing should soon settle the question satisfactorily. If this suggests that all the flies would do better at a rather greater depth, it may then be necessary to treat the last yard of the line with fuller's-earth to make it sink. Now it will probably also be found that working the flies a little is more attractive than just allowing them to drift unchecked. Unfortunately this inevitably leads to missing more of the offers, but that position is quite acceptable so long as the intervals between hooking fish securely are not too great.

In similar conditions on those chalk streams where the rule is dry-fly and nymph only, upstream fishing with weighted nymphs is employed with notable success. A modified form of the sink and draw method is used. The idea is to make the nymph, near to the bottom, behave in a life-like manner. One of the great attractions of this style of fishing is that the bigger grayling take just as freely as the others.

With a favourable light, it may be possible to watch the nymph all the time and see the fish move to it. Then there is no problem concerning striking quickly enough. When the visual kind of fishing is not possible, the point where the cast dips beneath the surface has to be watched carefully and this gives the cue as to when to strike.

Oliver Kite covers this subject very fully and interestingly in his book 'Nymph Fishing in Practice', which I have mentioned earlier. These days Oliver uses only the one kind of nymph. It is actually no more than a bare hook with a bit of fine copper wire wrapped round the top of the shank. My understanding of his view is that the two primary factors are to get the nymph down quickly to the depth required and then to give it movement to simulate a living creature. Hence his faith in an extremely austere looking artificial. His catches are certainly big enough to prove his point. Nevertheless, knowing how fond grayling are of a bit of bright colour, I am inclined to favour taking advantage of any help it can give. Oliver created a dry-fly that he has named the 'Imperial'. I think that if he would tie a 'Union Jack' nymph, some of the grayling would appreciate the change of diet.

When strong wind makes upstream nymphing too difficult, the chalk-stream fisher turns round and fishes the weighted nymph across and down. Then it is practically the same as fishing the leaded fancy grayling flies.

Nymph fishing upstream will, of course, take grayling on rain-fed rivers, and when the whole procedure of the nymph approaching the fish and the subsequent take can be seen clearly, it is most fascinating. But because of the differences in character of the two kinds of river, the weighted nymph and the leaded fancy flies are each the most suitable for the waters for which they were originally devised.

On the chalk-streams when the grayling begin to shoal-up, the pockets of deeper, unobstructed, steadily flowing water which the fish then favour are of relatively limited dimensions, and the concentration of fish is often very dense. Anglers know these specific places well and they can drop their nymphs into the water with reasonable certainty that they will be covering fish every time.

Shoaling-up on the rain-fed rivers presents a variety of problems that do not occur on chalk streams. Firstly, the type of water which the shoals of grayling favour in this context is much more plentiful and the chances are that many places which are very suitable will be uninhabited at any one particular time. Therefore it is necessary to be able to make a quick and effective search of any selected stretch of river, and, with the fly-rod, the best answer is to fish a cast of leaded fancy flies across and down. Secondly, when a shoal has been discovered, it is quite probable that the position will not lend itself to the rather exacting requirements of upstream nymph fishing. It may be that the fish can only be reached adequately with longish, diagonal casts. Furthermore, the suitable area of water probably being comparatively large, the grayling will be spread out. These factors once again put a premium on the much bigger effective coverage provided by the leaded flies fished across and down.

Perhaps I should qualify the foregoing slightly by saying that as a matter of policy, I try to avoid any wading at all in winter. If I am fortunate enough to live to a ripe old age, I hope I shall be able to spend it on the riverside and not in an armchair crippled with rheumatism. I get my full share of wading most of the year round, and I don't want to tempt fate too much. However, there are undoubtedly places to be found on the rain-fed rivers where deepish wading would make upstream nymphing a sound proposition. Even so, one must search out the grayling first, and nymphing is not the way to do that.

In support of upstream nymphing on chalk-streams, I should have mentioned that with skilful fishing, the vital area where most of the offers are to be got is disturbed much less than would be possible with the across and down method. I suppose you could put it in a nutshell by saying that upstream nymphing is the intensive method, and wet-fly across and down the extensive way of fishing.

Some anglers are now using the relatively new fast sinking lines for wet-fly and nymph fishing. When there is a lot of difficulty in getting the artificial down far enough owing either to the strength of the current or the depth of the water, there would seem to be some advantage in this. My own very limited experience with this type of line, however, prompts me to warn the novice to avoid going to the river armed only with a fast sinker. Even quite late in the season, the grayling may be found to be favouring gentle flows of only very moderate depth, and there the heavy line goes straight to the bottom like a stone. Any other style of presentation than right among the pebbles is then virtually impossible.

Before leaving the subject of fly-fishing for the present, there is a point of which I personally have foolishly fallen foul on numerous occasions. It is very necessary to keep leaded flies, ordinary wet-flies, and all flies that are fished dry, entirely separate. It is a hopeless job trying to make a leaded Sturdy's Fancy float and an irritating nuisance when a Treacle Parkin that has once been greased gets inadvertently onto the wet-fly cast.

Long-trotting:
Equipment and Baits

Proficiency in long-trotting entails the effective presentation of the bait and the successful hooking of the fish at greater distances than in any other kind of river fishing, spinning included.

Some anglers whose performance is restricted by inadequate tackle, disbelieve the distances said to be achieved by experienced long-trotters. One day on the Wharfe, Terry Thomas and I were talking about this. Terry hooked a grayling opposite a tree, and although there was no suggestion that it was even approaching the maximum possible distance, the chance that the marker gave to get a reasonably accurate, verified figure was too good to miss. After the fish was netted, we paced it out and made it seventy yards. This gives some idea of what can be done.

The importance of being able to maintain effective control of the tackle for long distances, however, is not by any means a matter of the satisfaction that it might give as a feat in itself. When the initial problem in winter is to find a shoal of grayling, it may be necessary to do a thorough search of a great deal of potentially good water, and the cost in time must be as small as possible. Efficient long-trotting is the only method that will fully satisfy these requirements.

Any single item of equipment that is not fully suitable

can render the whole outfit quite useless as far as achieving reasonable distance is concerned. A close study of the tackle is necessary, therefore, if the angler is to equip himself satisfactorily at the first effort and avoid an expensive and frustrating period of trial and error.

The rod must have a very quick action. On the strike when a long length of line is out, the tip of the rod often goes well behind one's head by the time contact is made with the fish. If the rod is too supple, the recovery of the tip from the strike has a habit of causing the line to get tangled round the top few rings. Any rod that may suffer from this tendency must be ruled out immediately.

Long stand-off rings, spaced closely, are necessary so that the line will always run freely without touching the rod. The longer the rod, the better it is for controlling the line and striking quickly enough. There is no difficulty these days in finding rods that are as long as anyone wishes and yet are remarkably light for their footage. But one must be very cautious not to be deceived into settling for a rod that is extremely nice to handle for a few minutes, but proves to be too tiring for several hours of fishing. It is far better to be faced occasionally with the wish that the rod were a little longer than with the need to break off fishing when sport is still good because your arms and back are aching.

Few anglers can fish indefinitely with comfort with a rod longer than eleven foot, no matter how light it is, and this is especially true if a fixed-spool reel is used. In some kinds of float fishing when one can be seated, the strain caused by the leverage of the rod can be obviated by propping the button of the handle against the body. Then a twelve footer is very easily handled. But when you have waders and a waterproof jacket on, a collapsible landing net hanging at your side, a basket heavy with grayling suspended from your shoulder, and you are constantly on the move down the river, there is no way of minimising the fatigue if the rod is the slightest bit too hard on you.

Just recently I have been informed that an ultra light 13 feet fibre-glass rod is being developed on an entirely new system of construction. This promises to be a real breakthrough and may alter my present opinion about rod lengths. If the action proves to be right and it permits a full day's fishing without fatigue, my present shorter trotting rods will certainly go into immediate and permanent retirement.

The line must be considered next, because this also has an important influence on the choice of the type of reel to be used. I think it is safe to say that the best performance of all is given by braided white terylene of 1½ lb test. It causes a minimum of drag on the float and imposes no limit to the distance that can be trotted. In most lights it can be seen easily, making any necessity for mending quite obvious. It lifts from the water instantly when required and this facilitates both mending and striking. Stretch is negligible, thus making the hooking of the fish more positive, and terylene stands up to the inevitable shock treatment it suffers remarkably well. Thus the bold, massive strikes that must be made when the float is a long way off can be carried out with the minimum of risk. Furthermore, terylene is very durable and will last indefinitely. The best plan is to get a 200 yard spool and dress it very lightly with a silicone grease, which will probably never need to be repeated. If the last yard is discarded after each day's fishing, there should never be any breakages on fish, and the line should last for at least two seasons.

Braided terylene has three disadvantages. The most serious is that if you catch a lot of grayling on a long line, the wear on the rod rings is very heavy. Eventually the line would perhaps cut right through the wire, but long before that stage is reached, the sharp edges of the deep grooves that are made in the rings are a source of possible danger to the line. The rings should be examined regularly and replaced if they look at all doubtful. Next, braided terylene does not come off the drum of the fixed-spool reel as well as monofilament. The performance of the reel is not seriously impaired, but it is a point that must be mentioned. Lastly, in windy conditions the light terylene line tends to drift across the surface of the water excessively; thus constant care is needed to ensure that the belly on the line is not too great for the strike to be effective when a bite comes.

The behaviour of fine nylon monofilament at the actual reel when using the fixed-spool type is excellent in all respects: for casting, for feeding line to the float, and during recovery. And for trotting moderate distances, it is reasonably good. But there are several shortcomings when a very long line has to be trotted. Unless the recently introduced fluorescent variety is used, it is often impossible to see where the monofilament is lying on the water and the need to mend the line cannot be anticipated: the drag has to show on the float first. Then it is found when the mend is being made that the line seems to cling to the water, and this pulls the float much further in the direction in which it was dragging. This makes it very difficult, if not impossible, to reach distances that are no problem with braided terylene. Furthermore, the clinging action of the monofilament tends to delay the effect of the strike, so that many bites are missed if and when the float can be made to travel beyond the moderate range. In windy weather, however, monofilament has the advantage that it does not drift across the water anything like as badly as braided terylene.

The characteristics of the two types of line nearly always result in the fixed-spool reel being loaded with monofilament and braided terylene being used on the centre-pin.

It cannot be denied that majority opinion, as judged by the outfits that are to be seen at work on the river, favours the fixed-spool reel. But it is equally true to say that sooner or later the majority of dedicated long-trotters opt for the centre-pin and braided terylene. Admittedly, on small rivers with shortish pools, the fixed-spool and monofilament will do all that is wanted. However, there are other factors concerning the two reels that should be considered before a final decision is made.

The fixed-spool has decided advantages in making long casts and a minimum of practice is required to become proficient. Also in the initial stages of the trot, the line feeds off the spool very easily: there is little risk of the float being held back any more than might be wished. The way the rod has to be held, however, with the reel bracket between the fingers, and with the forefinger poised ready to drop on to the spool and trap the line when a strike is made, is very tiring. The rod soon begins to feel heavy, and in cold weather the fingers of the right hand are very vulnerable.

Some apprenticeship must be served with the centre-pin before a long two or three loop cast can be made without getting tangles. Also, it is by no means easy to feed the line quickly enough immediately after the cast to keep pace with a fast current. When the float has travelled ten or 15 yards, the pull on the line helps the feeding process and there should be no further difficulty. If the rod is held above the reel, with the side of the little finger touching the rim and acting as a brake, the fingers are kept close together and this is a help against the hand getting uncomfortably cold. Also, the lower part of the rod handle is then supported beneath the forearm and this is certainly the least tiring way to fish. The best type of centre-pin for long trotting has a fairly heavy, metal

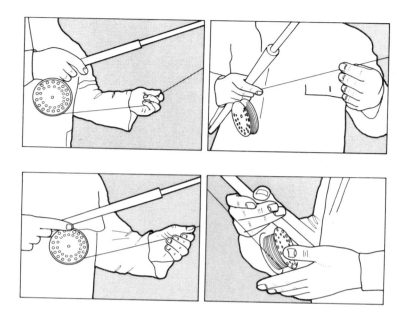

Top left: Paying line from the centre-pin reel with the little finger of the right hand acting as a brake on the rim.

Top right: In windy weather it is an advantage to feed the line through the forefinger and thumb of the right hand, while also checking the reel with the little finger.

Bottom right: Recovering line by batting with the left hand, but still controlling the reel with the edge of the little finger.

Bottom left: A popular method of controlling the centre-pin reel. This is more tiring, and less comfortable for the forefinger in cold weather.

drum which will continue to revolve for a long time after one tap of the hand. This makes the recovery of the line very easy. If the drum is too light, the hard batting that has to be done to get the line back is very laborious. About four inches is the most convenient size.

It will be seen that to recommend either type of reel to the exclusion of the other would be too onerous. Yet if the novice possesses both kinds, there is a danger that he will never practise with the centre-pin enough to become proficient with it: in my opinion, that would be a pity. The fixed spool will almost certainly produce more grayling for him in his early days, but mastery of the centre-pin is a very definite necessity if the maximum benefit is to be got from all the good opportunities that will arise in a winter's fishing.

As with the other items of equipment already mentioned, it is very necessary to appreciate the details of the performance required of the float. In the order in which it will be fished, it needs enough weight for a long cast to be made easily. The balance should ensure that it will turn over once, and once only, during the cast, thus avoiding any tendency to get tangled and inverted on the line. It must have enough buoyancy to carry the shot and bait in fairly rough water; draw the line along behind it without being held back too much; withstand mending without losing its course in line with the current; be easily visible at a long distance; and yet be sufficiently sensitive to register a bite positively and unmistakably.

Traditional style grayling floats, of course, have many shortcomings in respect of these modern requirements. But they must be mentioned first because some anglers apparently think they have rather magical qualities. The cob floats are the most famous of the old designs and will suffice for fishing small pools provided one is familiar with their peculiar performance. A bite does not necessarily pull the float under the surface – in fact it rarely does so. Often there is just a sideways movement, or the float simply stops in its track. Soon one gets used to striking at any action that does not seem to be in conformity with unrestricted movement along with the current. But it must be repeated that in the context of present day long-trotting concepts, the old fashioned floats are decidedly inadequate.

An ordinary bob float is perhaps as good as anything on the market for long-trotting, but it still leaves much to be desired. It is too difficult to see at a long distance and unless it is over-shotted – which makes it even more difficult to see – it is not sufficiently sensitive always to register bites quickly enough. The fish feels the resistance of the float and lets go before the hook is driven home.

The lack of a really good, practical grayling float became apparent to me many years ago. I started experimenting with all sorts of ideas to try and get an arrangement that would enable me to exploit fully the excellent capabilities of the rest of the equipment. Eventually I began to make slight progress and then due to one line of research that produced exactly the opposite effect to what I had hoped for, I hit on the principle that was wanted to solve the problem. The first efforts on the new basis were very encouraging and, after some refinements, the float fulfilled all requirements better than I had ever dared to hope. For the past ten to 15 years it has been gaining in popularity and is now widely used by grayling enthusiasts.

As the illustration in Appendix B shows, (see Fig. 6, page 115), an elongated bulb merges into an antenna above, and is mounted on a long fine stem below. The materials are balsa wood and mild steel wire. The stem acts as a keel and the float is self-cocking. With one or two shot on the cast, it floats with the antenna only above the surface. The long stem ensures that the antenna remains practically upright in all reasonable conditions. If fluorescent paint is used, it can be seen clearly in most lights at any distance that is ever required. During recovery, the streamlined shape enables the float to slide along the surface with a minimum of disturbance, which is pleasing compared with the way bob floats kick up and down and perhaps upset the fish.

Unfortunately there is no commercial supply of these floats. However, they are not difficult to make and full details are given in Appendix B.

Eric Horsfall Turner has produced a modified form of the float that is very suitable for the small pools on the upper Yorkshire Derwent. I have seen other variations recently that are not so good, chiefly with a shorter stem. I think this is a mistake, because the long stem is no disadvantage in any respect, while to shorten it reduces the leverage that holds the float vertical. Also, the longer the stem, the more positive and smooth is the turnover in the air when the cast is made.

The three lb nylon used for points of fly casts is excellent for trotting casts. It is a good plan to ensure that they are no longer than the depth of the shallowest water that is likely to be fished, so that the float will always be on the reel line. The reason is that if the hook gets fast on the bottom, any breakage that might occur will usually take place where the cast is tied on to the line. It does not matter much if the hook length is lost, but it is a pity to lose the float as well when this can be avoided so easily. A length of the reel line below the float when fishing the deeper swims is no disadvantage, and therefore there is no call for the cast to be longer than about two feet at the most.

Hooks can be a serious let-down. On one occasion I had landed several grayling without any trouble on crystal bend hooks whipped to nylon. Towards dusk I came across a shoal of big fish in a very solid flow of water. They took the gilt-tail readily, but fish after fish straightened out the hook, which, of course, I had renewed in each case. It was impossible to move down and get opposite the hooked fish, but apart from that, I did everything I knew without it making any difference – the fish won every time. This shook me into adopting the practice of some other Wharfe grayling fishers – the use of eyed fly hooks tied on to the cast with a double turle. Wide gape, up-eyed hooks of the best quality have proved very satisfactory, but even with these it is necessary to test a sample from each new supply. The temper of some may be rather on the soft side. Also, the barb must be checked every time a grayling is unhooked: one must be prepared to replace the hook several times in a day's fishing. To save time, I keep a supply in a small pill bottle with a snap-on plastic top. This is always in my pocket with the scissors and the changing of a hook is no more than a minute's job.

The sizes of hooks required vary according to the state of the river and the bait used. With the gilt-tail hooked on as I shall describe shortly, 14s are advisable in a big or coloured water, but 16s are plenty big enough in normal conditions.

The last important item of equipment I should like to mention here is the polaroid glasses. If the sun at its low winter angle is shining straight up the pool, the glare makes it difficult if not impossible to follow the float any distance with the naked eye. While on this subject, it should also be mentioned that after the sun has gone down on a day when the light has been good, the float can be seen for a much longer period if one can fish facing approximately South West and not the other way.

Experienced grayling fishers are mostly agreed that a small red worm, preferably the gilt-tail or cockspur, is the best bait. Maggot will, of course, catch a lot of fish, and with maggots so readily available, some anglers think it too much trouble to bother about worms. But the advantages of the gilt-tail and the disadvantages of the maggot are very considerable. The maggot being seemingly a small and insignificant bait (whereas in fact it is quite a sizeable morsel to a grayling) most anglers think it necessary to throw a few into the water as feeders. Certainly this can soon get the grayling on the look out for more and can hold a shoal of fish together. The trouble is that it can also bring the trout on to the

The Wharfe between Burnsall and Grassington. The glide below the trees on the far side is equally good for dry-fly fishing or trotting, according to the height of the water. *(Don Peacock)*

A magnificent dorsal fin. On numerous photographs of grayling by different photographers I have noticed white marks on fins and tails, similar to the ones here; I think they must be drops of water. *(Roy Shaw)*

At the head of the pool at Loup Scaur on the Wharfe: Eric Horsfall Turner hooking a grayling on trotting trackle. *(Arthur Oglesby)*

Grayling of 2 lb 2 oz and 1 lb 1 oz, taken on gilt-tail from the upper Yorkshire Derwent and on the Wharfe respectively on two consecutive days by Eric Horsfall Turner. Note the spiked dorsal fin of the larger fish and the relatively small difference in the length of the two. *(Eric Horsfall Turner)*

The late T. K. (Tim) Wilson on his local stretch of the Aire near Skipton. *(Arthur Oglesby)*

The Yore at Bainbridge, high up the dale. *(Edward Hinchliffe)*

Left: The late Oliver Kite surveys Wylye. The smooth water in background is a favourite spot for grayl (*Peter W. Dickenson*).

Right: The Kennet (*Bernard Venab*

Roy Shaw – well known for his unique photographic record of grayling during the spawning period – playing a Yorkshire chalkstream grayling. (*Charles Derrick*)

A cage of grayling about to be released into the Aire near Keighley. The fish came from the Costa Beck. *(Edward Hinchliffe)*

Grayling from the Driffield Beck being turned into the Driffield Canal. The canal is fed by water from chalk springs. Grayling maintain a rapid rate of growth in this new home. *(Roy Shaw)*

A good high stretch of water for trotting, on the Wharfe below Grassington. *(Arthur Oglesby)*

The Swale below Gunnerside. *(Michael Pritchard)*

The mouth of a northern grayling. Note the length of the lower jaw. *(Roy Shaw)*

Terry Thomas with trotting tackle on the Yorkshire Derwent. *(Eric Horsfall Turner)*

The Wharfe at the bridge near Bolton Abbey. *(Arthur Oglesby)*

The Wharfe at Loup Scaur. Note the long stand-off rings on the author's trotting rod. Only the two bottom rings are porcelain lined. *(Arthur Oglesby)*

The Yorkshire Derwent in Forge Valley. Arthur Oglesby playing a grayling in a delightful pool. *(Eric Horsfall Turner)*

Len Stott fly fishing on the Yore at Bolton Hall.

Grayling taken on fly after the turn of the year. *(Leonard Stott)*

The late T. K. Wilson with a grayling from the river Aire at Skipton. *(Michael Pritchard)*

Top and centre: Grayling fishing on the river Wharfe in winter.
Bottom: Dr. Ian Calvert-Wilson fishing the Yore. *(Arthur Oglesby)*

feed. Even when the temperature of the water is low and the digestion of the trout dormant, maggots thrown in as feeders are too big a temptation and they start moving. Needless to say, this is just what the angler does not want to happen, because of both the nuisance and the risk of the grayling then departing.

If any grayling fisher lacks confidence that the small red worm trotted down the river entirely on its own is sufficient attraction for the fish, the results achieved on the waters of the Appletreewick, Barden and Burnsall Club on the Wharfe should be convincing enough. The rules forbid the use of feeders and the long-trotting done is almost entirely with the gilt-tail. Each generation of members seems to include one outstanding grayling fisher whose idea of a day's fishing is to search the rivers for miles from first to last light. For some years, Jack Aykroyd has been the name that one is always hearing about. He considers the grayling to have been in a quiet mood if his catch is anything less than 20 fish: double that number would be required before he would say that sport had been brisk. And since Jack's best catches have been a long way in excess of the half-century, it will be appreciated that his idea of what can be called good sport is not by any means immodest.

Members who take their fishing much more casually can often land twenty grayling on a good day, but what is the most important thing in the present context is that you could never get one of them – the anglers, not the fish – to look at a maggot again.

From time to time people have told me that grayling elsewhere are not so keen on the gilt-tail as the Wharfe fish. My experience has been that it has killed just as well in every river where I have tried it. Furthermore, in unfamiliar waters I have followed behind other anglers baiting and feeding with maggot and the gilt-tail has not failed to produce pleasing comparisons; and, incidentally, win enthusiastic converts.

The reasons for the gilt-tail monopolising my mention so far of small red worms are numerous. The brandling is probably not much less desirable to the grayling, but it has the tendency to stretch out in the water to a great deal more than its normal length. If the fish are keen, this does not matter much as far as they are concerned: one good suck and the whole worm goes right into the mouth with amazing speed. But the trouble then is that on the strike, the hook is more likely to re-enter the worm at another point than to penetrate the jaw of the fish. The gilt-tail can stretch itself a little but that does not happen often and certainly not to any troublesome extent.

If the gilt-tail is hooked on by the smallest, shallowest amount possible at the back of the head, it retains its normal length and swishes its tail about for long enough. Many people think that the coloured tip of the tail wagging about energetically is particularly attractive to the grayling.

When the fish are feeding at all well, most of the bites will result in good hook-holds. Occasionally the hook will re-enter the worm and pull away: some fish will be lost through being hooked in the tender part of the mouth, (more about this later); and odd grayling will steal the worm with impunity. Nevertheless, one could not wish for a better bait. Details concerning the gathering and keeping of gilt-tails appear in Appendix C.

Long-trotting:
Practical Problems

The observance of a few simple rules for shotting the cast can save a lot of inconvenience.

Any tendency for the bait to get hung up on the line above the float when casting can be avoided by ensuring that the distance from the hook to the shot is always smaller than that from the shot to the float. In this respect, one large shot heavy enough to balance the float would be satisfactory; but to make it easier to effect the adjustments that are certain to be required from time to time, my method is to have the necessary weight divided into two shot of about the same size. These are pressed gently on to the cast so that they can be made to slide up and down the nylon.

In normal swims of two to three feet deep, the two shot are kept together, ten to fourteen inches from the hook. In deeper water, it is an advantage to have the shot spread on the cast. This gives a smoother action when casting and helps the float to ride more steadily during the trot. Therefore one shot is left in position and the other is slid about a foot up the cast.

No shot is likely to be required on the operative part of the cast in swims of less than two feet deep. The float is placed in the required position, say eighteen inches from the hook, and the two shot are run up the nylon to the end of the float. This saves all the trouble of removing shot and substituting a fully self-cocking float. Much care is now needed to ensure that the bait does not get caught above the float when casting: that risk is present whatever system is used when there is no weight between the bait and the float.

Sliding the shot on the nylon does not harm it at all. It may be necessary occasionally to give the shot another very gentle squeeze if they slip a little when casting or striking, but this is a small penalty for the benefits that the two-shot system gives.

The next question is the depth at which the bait should be fished in relation to the bottom. One hears it said at times that minute adjustments to the position of the float can make the difference between good sport and failure. I am certain that this idea should not be taken too seriously. When you consider the irregularities in depth of any swim and the variations in the way the turbulence of the current carries the bait – lifting it a little here and dropping it there – it becomes clear that fishing at a calculated, precise distance from the bottom is a physical impossibility. Furthermore when the grayling are moving at all well, they show a great willingness to rise quite a way to take a bait. And, as will be explained shortly, there are considerable advantages in having fish come up a little way for the gilt-tail as opposed to their taking it without moving from the bottom.

The first thing to do, then, is to establish by trial and error the length of cast that just allows the whole swim to be trotted without the float being pulled down by the bait fouling the bottom. One can then be sure that if there are grayling present that are in a feeding humour, there will be no failure to get bites. If these result in secure hook-holds in the upper jaw, it is unlikely that any improvement could be made at this juncture. But if several grayling are hooked and lost, as sometimes will be the case, the cast should be shortened by two or three inches at a time until fish are brought to the net satisfactorily. The reason for poor hook-holds in the tender parts of the sides of the mouth is that if the cast is too long in relation to the depth of the water, the strike tends to draw the hook horizontally instead of upwards.

It must be acknowledged that when the grayling are in an indifferent mood, the best chance of an odd fish or two taking the bait is when it is trundling along the bottom past their noses. But this is certainly not the way to make a good basket during the periods when the fish are feeding well: then it is preferable to make the grayling come up at least six inches to get the gilt-tail. Not only does this result in the float going under with a bang when the fish takes and usually in a secure hook-hold, but also it increases the chance of getting a bite in the first place. A bait very close to the bottom can easily escape the notice of a fish that is lying a little way off the line of travel. But if the bait is nicely clear of the bottom, more grayling have the chance to see it as it approaches and move into position to intercept it without too much effort. This also applies in a coloured water. When the range of visibility of the fish is restricted, there is an understandable tendency on the part of the angler to think that it is an advantage to get the bait down as near to the fish as possible. This is, of course, a wrong appreciation. The bait stands out much better against the source of light up above than it does when seen along a horizontal line of sight. If any doubt remains, think of the grayling moving up through coloured water to take a dry-fly on the surface: the gilt-tail a little way above the fish must make a far greater impact.

Now comes a question which causes quite a lot of controversy. I should say that perhaps the majority of anglers consider that the float should invariably be held back, at least very slightly, in all cases when trotting. In most situations, I disapprove of this entirely.

The main, if not the only, exception I would make is in water of greater depth than four or five feet where there is a very heavy flow. There some checking of the float is essential to prevent the bait from dragging behind and consequently fishing further from the bottom than is wished in the circumstances. But on the northern grayling streams, it is rare to find the fish in such places. Their normal preference is for steadier water if it is deep, and shallower water if it is very fast. Anglers who check their floats in those two kinds of water do so with the idea of making the bait travel ahead of the tackle, which they believe to be the most attractive presentation. But the character of such swims and the type of shotting used make it questionable whether the delicacy required to check the float effectively can be achieved regularly and reliably without the risk of causing other, unwanted results, such as the bait being pulled up too high in the water and excessive drag. However, even if this manoeuvre can be accomplished correctly, it cannot be a vital matter because large numbers of grayling are caught regularly by allowing the float to travel as fast as the current will take it. Now, concerning this question of drag: if the current is not able to take a drifting article along with it at its own speed, the force of the water automatically pushes the object aside in the direction of the slacker flow. Thus any attempt to check the speed of the float must tend to create drag and cause, among other things, a big reduction in the distance that can be trotted.

Jack Aykroyd, whose opinion must be respected in view of the tremendous catches of grayling he makes, is almost fanatical in his belief that the best response can only be got when the bait is moving in strict conformity with the line of the current that carries it. For that reason, he hates any wind that may cause drag and he is always willing to wade deeply in the coldest water if it will help him to control the float so that it will not depart from the true line of the flow. Personally I am satisfied that the grayling are not altogether as fastidious as that implies. Nevertheless, there can be no argument about avoidable drag not being wanted because, in effect, the whole art of long-trotting depends on successfully overcoming the many influences that cause drag.

By the way, if by wading, or finding a suitable set in the current, the float can be trotted down directly from the rod point, care must be taken when retrieving the float to keep it clear of the area being fished. A small object floating on the surface at the speed of the flow does not worry the grayling, even in very shallow water. But the same thing continually racing upstream above their heads cannot be expected not to disturb them.

In two situations there are advantages in deliberately holding the float back quite a lot, but this should not be confused with the habitual slight checking that I have been at pains to discourage.

Firstly, when the float has reached the limit to which it is intended to go in the particular swim, it is a good manoeuvre to cease paying out line and hold the rod quite still for a few moments before commencing to recover line. As the float gradually comes to a halt, the current sweeps the gilt-tail upwards and this is often extremely tempting to the fish. Sometimes, although no indication has been given by the float, when the line is tightened a grayling is felt to be there. In such a case, it may be too late to strike before the fish lets go. Nevertheless, it is remarkable how many fish are caught right at the end of the trot by the lifting of the bait.

The second kind of situation when retarding the float quite a lot may succeed is where there is a very strong flow in a shallowing, accelerating glide, at the tail of a pool. This is especially so when big grayling are lying near partly submerged boulders or clumps of long, trailing strands of weed. The float is set to give a distance to the bait of 18 inches to two feet greater than the average depth of the water. After casting, the float is held hard for a moment while the cast swings round and then line is paid out at considerably less than the speed of the current. It must be acknowledged that this lacks the precision of normal trotting. Often there is very little indication from the float when the gilt-tail has been taken. Nevertheless, some grayling are caught in this way after the ordinary method has failed. Perhaps it is the showy way in which the gilt-tail wavers to and fro in the vicinity of the lies that makes the difference that tempts the fish. On the other hand, it could be simply a matter of the time factor, in that the grayling have a longer opportunity to move and intercept the bait.

An adaptation of this method can sometimes be useful if the river is very low and the fish are lying in water that is too slow for satisfactory trotting. With the float set at about one and half times the depth of the water, a long throw is made at about 45° to the flow. Before the bait has had time to settle fully, the line is inched in so that, combined with the slight current, it makes the float describe a big arc. Of course, the grayling have to be pretty hungry for this to work well, but I have seen Arthur Oglesby make a fine catch when the circumstances gave him little alternative than to cover practically the same area of water with every cast.

There are several other alternative ways of presenting the bait, such as laying-on, stretting and light ledgering, which may tempt a few fish when they are rather indifferent. But trials with orthodox trotting should always be carried out at regular intervals to check whether the fish have made one of their unpredictable changes of mood. One can easily be led into the belief that the latest variation from trotting to be tried has solved a difficult problem, when, in fact, the problem has disappeared, the fish having become readily responsive.

On most occasions when the grayling show any real interest in the gilt-tail, they take it very solidly. Now and again however, it seems that they cannot resist plucking at the bait although they are not keen enough to take it properly. When this happens, the first thing to be tried is to avoid the slower swims and see if fish can be found in pretty fast water. If the grayling are taking at all there, it is nearly certain that they will get hold securely. Should that fail and one be compelled to attempt to cope with the position in the steadier flow, the answer may be that the smallest gilt-tails that can be found, say about half an inch long, will put an end to the difficulty.

However, this curious, unserious interest in the bait nearly always proves to be the prelude to very good sport a little later, especially during the last hour of daylight. It pays therefore to submit to the teasing by the grayling and not to reach too hasty a conclusion that fishing on is going to be useless.

Lastly, netting a big grayling in fast water can be made a much more difficult problem than it needs to be. If the fish is brought in close to the bank below the angler, this results in the attempt to net it being made on the downstream side, which puts enormous strain on the rod and tackle. If there is any weakness in the hook-hold, the fish will be lost. At the best, the fish on the short line flops about on the top of the water before it is quite reachable and altogether the performance looks very inexpert. On the other hand, when the fish is being brought up the pool towards the angler, it always tries to bore outwards and if the rod tip is kept pointing straight out and at an angle of about 45°, the fish will continue upstream past the angler, against the strain of the shortening of the line and the strong current. When the grayling is three or four yards upstream of the angler, the rod is drawn gently but firmly towards the bank while the line is further shortened. Then the net is placed in position and the raising of the rod to the vertical brings the fish down with the current and into the net without any commotion. The only slight criticism that could be made against this method is that the grayling goes tail first into the net, but in these particular circumstances it is most unusual for this to result in any disastrous acrobatics by the fish.

Conditions for Long-trotting

Many grayling fishers – probably the majority – will tell you that the best catches with long-trotting are made in autumn when the river is at a good height; also that soon after the Christmas period sport falls off particularly badly and that from then onwards it is usually very disappointing.

Yet there is a popular belief – very much justified – that the grayling become hungriest and keenest when a spell of extremely hard weather has got firmly established. This is most likely to occur in January or February, and just a few stalwarts assert that these are the months that can produce the fastest sport of the season. So, what is the answer?

The truth undoubtedly hinges on the fact that the very coldest weather (not immediately after the change from milder conditions) does indeed make the grayling extremely eager to take bait, but it also makes them huddle very closely together in tight shoals. And these can be exceedingly difficult to locate compared with earlier in the season.

In order to consider this situation in its full context, it is necessary to trace the trend of all the movements of the grayling, commencing in the summer months. These migrations, so to speak, are not, of course, dictated solely by the reactions of the grayling to the changes in their own physical condition and in their environment. The habits of the trout have an important bearing on the selection of lies by the grayling, which must – my apologies for the repetition – almost always accept second choice. This makes it necessary to begin with some observations about the trout. Once the spring hatches of fly have put the trout into good condition and they have energy to spare, they spread out and occupy every kind of good feeding lie, both in broken water and in smooth glides. For the sake of later reference, it is well to recognise here that the occupants of glides have much harder work to do than fish that are lying in turbulent water. If you have any doubts on this point, watch a trout feeding on floating duns in a glide. It remains just a few inches below the surface so that it can push up its nose and suck in flies in quick succession. But all the time it has to swim hard – at the speed of the flow – to do this. If you look at its tail and fins, you will see that they never stop working. In more turbulent, popply water, a trout feeding similarly on the surface again remains high in the water, but it uses the variations in the current to do for it most of the work of maintaining position. It is easy to see that the trout sways to and fro with the ever changing, helpful bit of turbulence: the tail and fins have to make only a fraction of the effort necessary in a glide.

In these warm months, the grayling have very little appetite and being so nervous of the trout, they are inclined to keep out of the way entirely. On many rivers that are well stocked with grayling, trout fishers can go through the best part of the season without ever seeing a grayling, never mind catching one. That may be why some 'trout-only' anglers imagine that grayling fishers suffer from mass hysteria and never really make the big catches later in the year that are heard of so often.

This seclusion of the grayling in summer carries on until the approach of the end of the trout season, or soon after the close. Then three major changes take

FISHING AND SPORTING
BOOKS AT BARGAIN PRICES

BARGAIN GUN BOOKS. .... INCLUDING 1997 EDITIONS!
1997 or 1996 GUN DIGEST. Large format Pbk. (£17.99) £4.95
1997 or 1996 GUNS ILLUSTRATED. Large format Pbk. (£14.99)...............................£4.95
1997 or 1996 SHOOTER'S BIBLE. The world's standard firearms reference book. Large
format Pbk. Price-guide for sporting guns & handguns in dollars. (£14.95) £4.95
GUN DIGEST TREASURY. The best of 45 years of Gun Digest. Large format Pbk. £4.95
HANDLOADERS DIGEST 1994. Large format Pbk. (£16.95)................................£4.95
PRACTICAL GUNSMITHING. Large format Pbk. (£14.99)..................................£4.95
THE SHOTGUN: HISTORY & DEVELOPMENT. Geoffrey Boothroyd. Hbk. (£19.99).................£9.95
BOLT ACTION RIFLES. Large format Pbk. (£17.99).......................................£7.95
KNIVES 1996 or 1997. Large format Pbk. (£14.99) £7.95

BARGAIN SPORTING BOOKS.
THE BOOK OF THE WOODCOCK. Colin McKelvie. Hbk. (£18.95) £12.95
MORE TALES OF THE OLD COUNTRYMEN. Brian P Martin. (£17.99)................£12.95
THE COUNTRY NATURALIST'S YEAR. McKelvie & Rodger McPhail. Hbk. (£19.95).........£7.95
THE GLORIOUS GROUSE. Brian P Martin. Hbk. (£17.99).............................. £9.95
WITH GUN, RIFLE & BOW: Stories for the field sportsman. James Douglas. Hbk. (£15.99) £5.95
TICKNER'S PONIES. Hbk. (£4.95)..£2.95
SPORTING PIGEON SHOOTING. Michael Brander. Hbk. (£8.95) £3.95
DEBRETT'S BOOK OF GAME CARDS. Lord Ralph Percy. Hbk. (£8.95)....................£3.95
BADMINTON LIBRARY: SHOOTING MOOR & MARSH. Hbk. (£16.95)......................£7.95
FUR, FEATHER & FIN SERIES. THE RABBIT, OR THE PHEASANT. (£15.95).......£5.95
A GUIDE TO AIRGUN HUNTING. Arthur Shepherd. Pbk. (£5.95) £2.95
FURTHER COUNTRY MATTERS. Duff Hart-Davis. (£16.95) £3.95
PASTORAL SYMPHONY. Chapman Pincher. Sporting anecdotes. Hbk. (£16.95)........£5.95
TALES FROM THE GUN ROOM. Michael Paulet. Hbk. (£12.95)............................£2.95
COUNTRYWOMEN. Emma Ford. Hbk. (£14.99) £2.95
A SHOOTING ANTHOLOGY. Michael Brander. Hbk. (£16.95)..............................£2.95
THE GREY GOOSE WING. E.G.Heath. Hbk. Scarce Archery classic. ($39.95)..........£14.95

PUBLISHED BY COCH-Y-BONDDU BOOKS!
SALTWATER FLYFISHING: BRITAIN & NORTHERN EUROPE. Edited by Paul Morgan.
The first British book on flyfishing for bass, mullet, seatrout, cod & garfish. Hbk.........£19.95

REMINISCENCES OF A FALCONER. Major C.H.Fisher. (1901) A high-quality reprint of a
scarce and popular falconry book. Limited edition of 1000 copies. Hbk. £30.00

FALLOW DEER. Donald & Norma Chapman. New edn of scarce monograph. Hbk. ..£30.00

FLYFISHING FOR SAILFISH. John Reynolds. Pbk. The first book by a British angler on this
new but rapidly growing sport. £9.95

PRACTICAL PEST CONTROL IN THE COUNTRYSIDE. George Hogg. Hbk.......£14.95

THE ART OF LONG-NETTING. Harold Wyman. Long awaited hbk reprint..............£16.95

IRISH TROUT & SALMON FLIES. E.J.Malone. 1st paperback edition. £14.95

BARGAIN GAME-FISHING BOOKS.

MURIEL FOSTER'S FISHING DIARY. Hbk in presentation box. (£29.95) £9.95
A GUIDE TO RIVER TROUT FLIES. John Roberts. Pbk. (£14.95)..........................£7.95
MICROPATTERNS. Darrel Martin. Hbk. (£24.95)..£14.95
FLY TYING WITH SYNTHETICS. Phil Camera. Hbk. (£16.95)...........................£9.95
IN THE RING OF THE RISE. Vincent Marinaro. Hbk. (£18.95)..........................£9.95
CHALKSTREAM CHRONICLE. Neil Patterson. Hbk. (£17.95)...........................£9.95
FISHING REFLECTIONS. Reg Righyni. Hbk. (£18.95)..£5.95
PETER DEANE'S FLY TYING. Hbk. (£17.99)...£9.95
SMALLWATER TROUT FISHING. Charles Jardine. (£25) £9.95
SEA TROUT FISHING. Hugh Falkus. Hbk. (£35)...£19.95
SALMON FISHING. Hugh Falkus. Hbk. (£35)...£19.95
TROUT AND TERRESTRIALS. Lou Stevens. Pbk. (£12.95)...............................£4.95
IMPROVE YOUR FLYCASTING. Lou Stevens. Pbk. (£12.95)...........................£4.95
FLY PATTERNS: AN INTERNATIONAL GUIDE. Taff Price. Pbk. (£15.99).............£7.95
THE TROUT FLIES OF BRITAIN & EUROPE. John Goddard. Hbk. (£35)...............£19.95
THE WORLD'S BEST TROUT FLIES. John Roberts. Hbk. (£19.95).......................£7.95
TYING & FISHING THE NYMPH. Taff Price. Pbk. (£14.99)...............................£7.95
SALMON FISHING ON SMALL RIVERS. Charles Bingham. Hbk. (£25)..............£9.95
THE CAST. Ed Jawarowski. Hbk. (£25)..£9.95
THE FLY-CASTING HANDBOOK. Peter Mackenzie-Philps. Pbk. (£11.99)..........£5.95
THE ART OF SEA TROUT FISHING. Charles McLaren. Hbk. (£12.95)..............£5.95
THE SALMON RIVERS OF SCOTLAND. Mills & Graesser. Hbk. (£17.95)..........£7.95
THE ENGLISH CHALK STREAMS. Sidney Vines. Hbk. (£19.99).......................£9.95
TALES FROM THE ROD ROOM. Michael Paulet. Hbk. (£12.95)........................£2.95
RIVER TROUT FLYFISHING. Peter Lapsley. Pbk. (£9.99)..................................£5.95
FISHING SEASON. Rodger McPhail. Hbk. (£18.95)...£9.95
FISHING THE SCOTTISH ISLANDS. Roderick Wilkinson. Hbk. (£16.95)............£7.95
TROUT FROM THE HILLS. Ian Niall. Hbk. (£14.95)..£7.95
RESERVOIR TROUT FISHING WITH TOM SAVILLE. Hbk. (£14.99)...................£7.95
LIFE IN LAKES & RIVERS. Macan & Worthington. Hbk. (£12.95)....................£5.95
STILLWATER TROUT: A month by month guide. Brian Musgrove. Hbk. £7.95. Pbk. .£5.95
THE COLLECTOR'S GUIDE TO ANTIQUE FISHING TACKLE. Calabi. Hbk. (£29.95)...£14.95
TROUT FROM SMALL STILLWATERS. Peter Cockwill. Pbk. (£9.99)................£5.95
BLACK GNAT. John England. Hbk. (£14.95) N.Z. South Island trouting...................£4.95
TROUT. Gale, Moore & Gathercole. Hbk. Ecology / stillwater fishing. (£19.50)........£5.95
MY MOBY DICK. William Humphrey. Good American tale of a big trout. Hbk............£1.95
TROUT BUM. John Gierach. Pbk. (£9.95)...£4.95
SEX, DEATH & FLYFISHING. John Gierach. Pbk. (£9.95)...............................£4.95

BARGAIN COARSE & PIKE FISHING BOOKS

SEARCH FOR BIG CHUB. Tony Miles. (£19.95)...£9.95
IN PURSUIT OF BIG TENCH. Len Arbery. (£19.95) £9.95
BAZIL'S BUSH. Rob Maylin. Hbk. (£21.95)..£9.95
THE FIFTH BRITISH CARP STUDY GROUP BOOK. Hbk. (£16.95)....................£4.95
SUCCESS WITH BIG TENCH. Chris Turnbull. Hbk. (£14.99)...........................£5.95
MEGA-PIKE. Eddie Turner. Hbk. (£16.95)...£7.95
SUCCESS WITH PIKE. Barrie Rickards. Hbk. (£15.99) £7.95
PIKE: THE PREDATOR BECOMES THE PREY. John Bailey & Martyn Page. Hbk.
(£19.95)..£9.95

NEW FISHING BOOKS COMPLETE CATALOGUE AT http://www.fishing.org/bonddu/

SUCCESSFUL SEA TROUT ANGLING. Graeme Harris & Moc Morgan. Hbk. £25.00
FLYFISHING FOR SAILFISH. John Reynolds. Pbk...£9.95
THE SALMON & SEA TROUT FISHER'S HANDBOOK. Falkus & Greenhalgh. Hbk. £17.95
TROUT & SALMON RIVERS & LOCHS OF SCOTLAND. Bruce Sandison. Hbk......£19.99
TROUT & SALMON FLIES OF SCOTLAND. Stan Headley. Hbk. £20.00
THE TROUT & SALMON FLIES OF IRELAND. Peter O'Reilly. Hbk. £20.00
TROUT & SALMON FLIES OF WALES. Moc Morgan. Hbk.............................£20.00
BROOK & RIVER TROUTING. Edmonds & Lee. New high-quality limited edition.....£32.50

RARE & UNUSUAL FLY TYING MATERIALS: A NATURAL HISTORY.
Paul Schmookler & Ingrid V. Sils VOLUME TWO - BIRDS & MAMMALS. £80.00

TYING THE CLASSIC SALMON FLY. Michael D Radencich. Hbk........................£50.00
MATCHING THE HATCH: Stillwater, river & stream. Pat O'Reilly. Hbk. £12.95
SEA TROUT: How to catch them. Charles Bingham. Hbk. £19.95
NORTH COUNTRY FLIES. T.E.Pritt. New facsimile of 1886 edition. Hbk.................£25.00
TUBE & WADDINGTON FLY DRESSING. Ken Sawada. Pbk. Wonderful photo's. ..£25.00
JOHN GODDARD'S WATERSIDE GUIDE. New edition. Hbk. £12.95
HOW TO CATCH BIGGER PIKE. Paul Gustavson. Hbk. £16.95
THE COMPLETE BARBEL ANGLER. Roger Miller. Hbk. £19.95
CONFESSIONS OF A CARP FISHER by "BB". Hbk...................................£20.00
SOMEWHERE DOWN THE CRAZY RIVER. Paul Boote & Jeremy Wade. Hbk. £18.95
PIKE ON THE FLY. Reynolds & Berryman. Pbk....................................£12.95
CARP ON THE FLY. Reynolds, Befus & Berryman. Pbk. £12.95
FISHING BAMBOO. **New John Gierach book**. Hbk. £14.95

A FEW NEW SPORTING BOOKS.
TALES OF A RAT-HUNTING MAN. Brian Plummer. Hbk. £14.95
ROGUES & RUNNING DOGS. Brian Plummer. Hbk. £14.95
THE LURCHER: TRAINING & HUNTING. Frank Sheardown. Hbk. £18.95
GOOSE SHOOTING. Alasdair Mitchell. Hbk. £18.95
BRAND-NEW STICKMAKING BOOK. **STICKMAKING.** Leo Gowan. Pbk. £12.95
BOOTHROYD'S REVISED DIRECTORY OF BRITISH GUNMAKERS. Hbk. £25.00
BIRMINGHAM GUNMAKERS. Douglas Tate. Hbk...................................£35.00
THE HOUNDS OF HEAVEN. Willie Poole. Hbk. *Hunting in the Shires & war in Bosnia.* ...£14.95
THE ART OF LONG-NETTING. Harold Wyman. Hbk....................................£16.95
FALLOW DEER. Donald & Norma Chapman. Hbk. £30.00

BARGAIN BIG-GAME HUNTING BOOKS
JIM CORBETT'S INDIA. Pbk. (£7.95)...£3.95
AFRICAN ADVENTURE. Denis Lyell. Hbk. (£19.95) £9.95
RECOLLECTIONS OF WILLIAM FINAUGHTY: ELEPHANT HUNTER. Hbk. £7.95
THIRTYSEVEN YEARS OF BIG GAME SHOOTING IN COOCH BEHAR, THE DUARS,
AND ASSAM: A rough diary. The Maharajah of Cooch Behar. (£75)...........................£35.00
THE SPELL OF THE TIGER: MANEATERS OF THE SUNDARBANS. Sy Montgomery.
....Hbk. (£16.95)....£7.95   Pbk. (£9.95)....£3.95
RHINO ROAD: THE BLACK & WHITE RHINOS OF AFRICA. Martin Booth. Hbk.
(£17.95) £4.95
THE BIG GAME RIFLE. Jack O'Connor. Hbk. (£29.95)..............................£14.95

VISIT OUR NEW SHOP IN THE CENTRE OF MACHYNLLETH.
OPEN MONDAY TO SATURDAY .... 9.00am to 5.00pm.

1998 GAME FAIR SCHEDULE

Come and see us at the following shows: Bring your surplus books to sell or trade!

DUTCH FLYFAIR, ZWOLLE............. May 2-3rd   CHATSWORTH ANGLING FAIR... May 9-10th
FALCONER'S FAIR, OFFCHURCH .... May 23-24th   GILFORD CASTLE G/FAIR, N.I. ... May 30-31st
WELSH G/FAIR. LLANDEILO............ June 20-21st ..N. IRELAND GAME FAIR. .... June 26-28th
C.L.A. GAME FAIR. Stratfield Saye, Hants.................July 24-26th
SCOTTISH GAME FAIR. SCONE. ..... July 4-5th   LOWTHER HORSE TRIALS. ....Aug 7-9th
WARKS G/FAIR, RAGLEY HALL. ..... Aug 15-16th   FENLAND G\FAIR, QUY................. Aug 30-31st
CHATSWORTH COUNTRY FAIR..... Sept 5-6th   MIDLAND GAME FAIR.................Sept 19-20th

DEER-STALKING AND SPORT IN SCOTLAND.

DEERWATCH. Richard Prior. Pbk. (£12.95)...£5.95
TORRIDON. Lea McNally. Hbk. (£17.95)..£7.95
STAG AT BAY. The Scottish red-deer crisis. Michael Wigan. Pbk. (£12.95) £5.95
THE ILLUSTRATED SIX-POINTER BUCK. David Stephen. Hbk.
.... The story of a roe-buck. (£17.95) £5.95
THE HIGHLAND GAME: Life on Scottish sporting estates. G.Satterley. Pbk. (£12.95)................£5.95

SPORTING DOGS, HOUNDS & THE CHASE.

TRAINING THE ROUGHSHOOTER'S DOG. P.R.A.Moxon. Hbk. (£14.95)...............£7.95
SECRETS OF DOG TRAINING. Brian Plummer. Limp covers. (£5.99)......................£2.95
THE SHOOTING MAN'S DOG. David Hudson. Hbk. (£19.95) £7.95
LIFE'S A BITCH, by "Dido" (Chapman Pincher's labrador). Hbk. (£15.95)....................£5.95
THE GREAT HUNTS. Alistair Jackson. (£14.95)...£9.95
BEAGLING. Jeremy Hobson. (£12.95)...£5.95

WILDFOWLING

DAYS AND NIGHTS ON HUNTER'S FEN. John Humphreys. (£17.99).......................£7.95
WILDFOWLING: ONE WINTER'S TALE. Alan Jarrett. Hbk. (£12.95)....................£5.95
FOWLING FOR DUCK. Mike Swan. (£12.95)...£5.95
PETER SCOTT: PAINTER & NATURALIST. Elspeth Huxley. Hbk. (£17.50)............£5.95
COL. HAWKER'S SHOOTING DIARIES. Edited by Eric Parker. Slipcase. £9.95

BOOKS ON FALCONRY & BIRDS OF PREY.

REMINISCENCES OF A FALCONER. Major C.H.Fisher. (1901) A high-quality reprint of a
scarce and popular falconry book. Limited edition of 1000 copies. Hbk. £30.00
DESERT HAWKING: With a little help from my friends. Harry McElroy. Hbk. New edition,
completely rewritten. Handling coopers', red-tail & Harris hawks.. ....£55.00
UNDERSTANDING THE BIRD OF PREY. Dr Nick Fox. Hbk. £37.50
THE PEREGRINE SKETCHBOOK. C.F.Tunnicliffe. Hbk. (£19.95)............................£9.95
FALCONRY: CARE, CAPTIVE BREEDING & CONSERVATION. Jemima Parry-Jones.
Hbk. (£17.99)...£9.95
THE RED TAIL. Daniel Butler. Hbk. (£14.99) £2.95

COCH-Y-BONDDU BOOKS

Papyrus, Pentrehedyn Street,
Machynlleth,
Powys SY20 8DJ

VISA/MASTERCARD/SWITCH taken by phone.
Postage extra to £3 maximum...

PAUL MORGAN

Phone: 01654-702837
Fax: 01654-702857

email: omorgan@zetnet.co.uk
http://www.fishing.org/bonddu/

.... Overseas postage at cost.

place rather suddenly. For the obvious reason that development for spawning is now occurring rapidly, the trout is not wasteful with its energy. It concentrates mostly on the turbulent areas for its feeding, and avoids the smooth, fast, gliding water. Furthermore hatches of fly tend to become of shorter duration and occur mainly in the middle of the day, thus reducing the inducement for the trout to remain in lies which require them to do any more work than necessary. At the same time, the grayling are getting considerably more interested in food, and as they find the glides to be relatively secure from the menace of the trout, they take up residence in such places and get a reasonable share of the flies that are going.

Now the grayling are in small shoals, no suitable feeding place being neglected by them, and this remains so more or less until the next big phenomenon of the river and its inhabitants takes place in about the middle of November. Then several great changes occur simultaneously. The long nights and low angle of the sunshine when it manages to penetrate result in the water remaining permanently in the winter bracket of temperatures. Fly activity becomes negligible, the appetites of the grayling grow, and those of the trout diminish greatly or entirely disappear. Also the trout feel the urge to seek out the spawning becks and shallows: they virtually vanish from the scene as far as the grayling and the angler are concerned. This gives the grayling almost free range of the river in their search for food when conditions are suitable. But the many small shoals begin the tendency to merge into a few, widely separated, large shoals. In readiness for their needs in the worst winter conditions, these bigger shoals draw into parts of the river where there are areas of deep, steady water close at hand. Long stretches of continuous shallows cease to be of much interest to the grayling.

In early December in a normal year when the weather is not yet too bitter, a shoal of grayling may be thinly spread over quite a large area. But as the grip of winter gets firmer, the fish draw closer and closer together until in January, a great number can be concentrated in a remarkably small space, while vast adjoining stretches are entirely vacant. Also, from about the middle of December onwards, the trout may take any easy opportunity to retire from the shallow water of spawning areas and seek comfortable lies in deeper, steadier water, in which to await milder conditions that will bring the reappearance of food and the return of their appetites. Thus they begin to encroach on the winter homes of the grayling, and although the trout are now very dormant, their presence undoubtedly has some tendency to pen the shoals of grayling in their retreats.

Looking at the grayling season now from the long-trotting point of view, the prospects from mid September to mid November depend largely on whether or not there is much fly on the water. Flies are undoubtedly the most desirable of all foods to the grayling. When they can satisfy their growing but still only rather mild hunger with flies, they will ignore anything else. Occasionally the gilt-tail will interest them when there are just a few grayling rising, but not enough fly for more than an odd taste now and again. Jack Aykroyd then takes quite a delight in spotting rises and trotting his gilt-tail to the precise spot. Sometimes this produces a nice basket of fish, but by and large the chances with bait are poor when there is anything like a reasonable quantity of fly. Hence the fact that the most suitable conditions for long-trotting are when the level of the water is high.

The best results with the gilt-tail on the autumn spate are to be had when the water has fined down to the level that permits the grayling to move back into lies on the edge of the fast flows. Rises to fly may be seen here and there, but the high water seems to put a better edge on their appetites, and with the grayling well spread out and not too selective, bites can be expected at any point down long stretches of suitable water. Moderately paced swims of two to three feet deep are the easiest to fish and usually the most productive, but it is remarkable how fast a flow the grayling will sometimes choose. Any favourite glide should always be given a trial even if it looks to be going much too quickly. If grayling are to be caught in such water, their fight is really magnificent.

All fish having been driven from their regular lies during the height of the spate, one cannot avoid hooking a few trout when shortly afterwards, the level of the water is at its best for the grayling. Of course, in this case it has not the same sinister meaning as when the river is at normal level. Perhaps the extra water gives the grayling a better sense of security, but whatever the reason, the occasional trout does not interfere with sport with the grayling. Now can be seen one of the advantages that orthodox trotting with the gilt-tail has over other forms of bait fishing. Practically all the trout hooked can be played to the side, the thumb and finger run down the cast to the hook shank and the fish shaken off without touching them. If the occasional trout is not lip hooked, it is best to cut the cast without touching the fish. The hook is most unlikely to do any harm – certainly it is less dangerous than handling and disgorging the trout.

When the river drops to normal level again and temperatures are seasonable – in other words, when conditions are favourable for fly fishing – trotting is rather at a discount. It would be a very poor day, however, if the faster glides failed to yield a few grayling, especially towards the close of day.

The worst possible conditions for trotting in autumn are when there is a droughty period. The popular belief is that the rotting of the dead leaves strewn on the bottom of the river sickens the fish, and there is probably much truth in this assessment. The only chance of a fish then is where some constriction causes a deepish, narrow, fast flow that keeps the bed of the river clean. But even there fly is likely to do better than bait.

In a normal season, the first stages of the winter conditions, from about the middle of November until the end of the year, are the most consistently reliable for good sport with trotting. Now fishing can also be very good when the river is not carrying any extra water. With no long lasting reason for the grayling to be suffering any lack of appetite and the trout probably out of the way, any swim that carries the float and tackle nicely has a good potential.

At the same time, the grayling may not show continuous interest throughout the day. And apart from saying that the last hour or so of daylight is very often a feeding period, I can give no really dependable guides to help to judge when the grayling are the most likely to take well. The appearance of a little soft sunshine on an overcast day, or a calm spell after some wind, may have a specially good influence, but a sudden, blustery snow shower may do the same thing. I certainly cannot claim to know of any genuinely regular pattern in the way the grayling react to the ordinary seasonable weather that is met on what one would call a reasonably pleasant looking day for fishing. Of course, there are cases of that sort when I think prospects look good and others when I do not feel optimistic, but in the end, the only way to find out whether the grayling are interested in bait at any one particular time is to catch some.

I hope this does not sound discouraging. It is not intended to be so. Almost invariably on a temperate sort of day, the grayling will provide brisk sport sooner or later. And as one never knows when a quiet spell will suddenly give way to one of ready response, the position is always very interesting and usually ripe with excellent possibilities.

It continues to be good policy during this early winter period to search the pools wholly from top to bottom. The shoals of grayling move quite a lot and since it is impossible to make a reliable spot judgment as to the exact type of water they will favour at any one time, it is too risky to elect to fish, say, only the glides, and ignore the runs and streams. Furthermore, it often seems that if the fish choose a stream during the first half of the day, they will favour the smooth water later, and vice versa.

In any large pool containing a long stretch of water of much the same depth and flow, a shoal of taking grayling has a tendency to move slowly but steadily upstream. The angler locating the shoal will have fished the pool down to that point without response and will rightly have assumed that the water above the shoal was vacant. Later when bites in the productive part of the swim become scarce, he may think that the grayling have become cautious and need resting: indeed, that may be so. But there is also quite a chance that he is now only covering the tail end of the shoal, which has gradually moved up and passed him. The leading fish are often the bigger ones and they will have seen less of the tackle than the others. Therefore, when it seems that a retreat upstream is perhaps the way to re-establish contact, it is best to leave a good margin for error, ensuring that fishing is resumed nicely above the top limit of the shoal. It does not take long to work down the pool again and get a good idea of the new whereabouts of the fish.

Earlier in the season when the shoals were small and well spread out, one would rarely be tempted to fish a pool down a second time, since virgin water ahead would almost always seem to offer better prospects. In these early winter conditions, however, one is loath to leave a shoal of fish that has shown some interest. But, of course, the system for maintaining contact with grayling moving up a long stretch is not suitable for smaller pools and dubs. If the stretch of potentially good water containing the shoal is less than about two hundred yards, a good plan is to fish the whole of it down quickly with no more than two or three trots from any one stand, and to keep on repeating this drill for as long as sport continues. In a dub there is little alternative other than to concentrate on fishing from the most advantageous position and rest the swim for ten minutes every time bites begin to fall off.

Hard weather before the turn of the year can be quite a problem. A sudden change resulting in the atmosphere being colder than the water is nearly always very unfavourable and it takes varying lengths of time before the low temperature begins to boost the appetites of the grayling. The second day of the spell may be good, but more often it is the third day before the grayling settle down to a continuously hungry mood. Fortunately the reverse action of the weather does not seem to upset the grayling, provided there is not a lot of snow to melt. Snow-broth is generally regarded as being pretty hopeless, but some anglers claim to have made good catches of grayling when there was little doubt that the extra water was due to the surface run-off of melted snow. I should not like to have to commit myself on this point. First of all, unless there is an extremely rapid thaw of a great deal of snow after a long period of low temperatures, it is not possible to judge the extent to which the river is affected by genuine snow-broth. Secondly, when the river is above normal level in the depths of winter, it is very difficult to locate the grayling whatever the cause of the extra flow, and failure to catch grayling can never be accepted as absolute proof that they are refusing to take. Lastly, my own experience prompts me not to disbelieve that grayling have been caught whatever the circumstances.

By January the development of the grayling towards readiness for spawning is considerable. This may be quite an important influence in respect of the unmistakable urge of the shoals to remain extremely compact. It has already been mentioned several times that the great problem now is to find a shoal.

I believe that it is rare at this time of the year for the grayling to be disinterested in food for any length of time and provided the water is at a reasonable fishing level, one should never give up hope. It requires a certain amount of experience of any stretch of river before one becomes familiar with the likeliest places in which to expect to find the fish, but the problem should not be regarded with too much apprehension. The searching of the pools with the gilt-tail can be done speedily and is never a waste of time – it all helps to get to know the water better and can provide valuable guidance for the future. Also one may easily come across another rod catching fish and an experienced grayling fisher will always hand over his swim to anyone with a dry net. Additionally this provides the positive information that the fish are taking and showing a preference for the particular type of water.

In very general terms, steadily flowing water of four to six feet in depth offers the best prospects, but the main factor seems to be that there should be some such water close at hand. If the grayling are extremely hungry, they may forage through shallows no more than a few inches deep, but that type of water can be ignored if it is a long way from a suitable bolt-hole.

Unfortunately when sport is at its best, there is frequently the risk of trouble with rod rings getting frozen up, more so with braided terylene than with monofilament. I regret to say that despite trials with all sorts of ideas, I have never discovered any way of preventing this satisfactorily. Any grease that is put on the rings gets worn off in no time and, of course, it only requires one individual ring to go solid for the line to become locked. However, ridding the line and rings of ice manually at short intervals will often enable two or three brace of fish to be taken and then one can feel that the day has certainly not been wasted.

I have saved one point about trotting in January and February for the last because it can be invaluable and cannot be stressed too much. Even in arctic temperatures that have made fishing almost out of the question, I have often seen grayling rising to take an odd fly and, on one or two occasions, smutting. One solitary dimple on the surface can, of course, reveal the whereabouts of a big shoal of grayling, and that insight may pay good dividends both immediately and during many future visits to the river.

Long-trotting Episodes

If I were asked to tell the story in full detail of a big catch of grayling made on a perfect day when everything went right, I should have to search my memory hard. That is not because such occasions are rare: on the contrary, uncomplicated good sport is commonplace with both fly and bait. The difficulty is that the best days are not remembered individually but merge into a pleasant, gratifying, general picture of beautiful valleys and streams; bulging rises to the fly; floats darting away beneath the surface; the magnificent colouring of grayling against a background of snow or red-brown fallen leaves; the acceptability of the six-hour-old tea from the flask, sipped during a few minutes' cheerful gossip with another rod; and the delightful contentment during the unhurried trudge back to the road when another wonderful day on the river is ending with the darkness.

But there are some spells of sport with the grayling that are remembered over the years, practically down to the minute by minute progress of the occasion. The difference that brings such a day to mind so readily is that some typical grayling peculiarity made an extraordinary impact which never seems to loose its freshness.

Brief consideration in abstract of various features of the behaviour of grayling may not be very impressive, but when certain aspects take part in actual experiences, their significance is registered permanently. It is in the hope of passing on some of this extra emphasis that I relate the following episodes.

At Loup Scaur on the Wharfe, the river has cut a deep, narrow gorge through a ridge of limestone. It looks like a natural dam that has been breached. The pool below is one of the best and most interesting, also most beautiful, that I have ever seen.

For some 20 to 30 yards, the head of the pool is fast and shallow, running over a bed of solid rock. Then it deepens slightly and steadies in about the middle and all the way across to the left bank. In that half of the river, the flow is maintained at a very favourable fishing speed for a great distance. Close to the right bank at the end of the shallow head of the pool, there is a deep drop-off which causes a big, widening backwater that extends downstream for 50 yards or more according to the height of the river.

Near the lower end of the backwater, the river is extremely wide and all the current being over towards the far side, it cannot be fished effectively from this point. A very long cast might just about reach the flow, but with so much line lying on slack water, it is impossible to prevent the float from being swept aside immediately.

The stand on the right bank at the top of the backwater, however, is an ideal fishing position. The current can be reached without difficulty and providing a little care is taken in mending the line so that it does not belly into the backwater, the float will travel down and outwards in the direction of the flow for a tremendous distance. On a good day, bites can be expected at any point all the way down this very fine swim.

Before I arrived at Loup Scaur one beautifully calm, sunny winter day, with the river at a perfect level for trotting, I had fished several excellent places en route without a single bite. Practically all the water had been shaded by the very steep sides of the valley and the hills beyond, but this was nothing unusual during the afternoon in these parts and it never occurred to me that this could be very important when everything else seemed eminently favourable. In fact, I don't think that I consciously noticed that the top of this famous pool which I was about to fish was similarly shaded. And despite my failure up to that time, I made the first cast from the favourite stand with every expectation that there would be a bite before the float had travelled very far. But it sailed on and on and my hopes diminished as the length of the trot kept on growing. Eventually, a great distance down the pool, the fluorescent red of the float became very much brighter. It had entered a rather small, sun-lit patch: the only such area, I then noticed, within my view. Two or three yards further on, the float suddenly slid under the surface. A tremendous sweep with the rod, while stepping backwards and drawing a big loop of line with the left hand, was necessary to make contact, but the grayling was well hooked. It takes quite a time to bring a fish to the net from such a distance, but once that was done, the float was on its way again without delay.

With this evidence of the presence of grayling and that they were not off the feed, I felt sure that a bite would come much sooner this time. But again a great length of very good water proved disappointing and when the float reached the sunshine for the second time, I really no longer had the slightest expectation that there would be another bite. It was a very pleasant surprise when the float went under and the second grayling was hooked.

It required four grayling to be taken from the same sunny spot with the four trots that succeeded in reaching it – two or three times the float ended up short in the slack at the side of the current – before the realisation came upon me that a shoal had, in fact, chosen to lie in the sunshine.

I should then have liked to cast from a point much nearer to the taking place in order to save the time wasted while the float was negotiating the long, unproductive part of the swim. But as I have explained, I was fishing from the only position on my side of the river that would permit the area in question to be covered effectively.

After a few more grayling had been taken in exactly the same manner, Jack Aykroyd joined me. On his way down the river, he had tried all the swims I had fished and with the same lack of response. I told him very enthusiastically about the sun-lit patch and invited him to test it for himself. It was quite an occasion when his float got to the right place and did the expected thing. Jack had a few more trots and he too never failed to get a grayling whenever he reached the sunshine.

The unshaded area was then narrowing and so that we could both make the most of the remaining opportunity, Jack waded out a long way across the fast, shallow neck of the pool and our floats began trotting down the swim side by side. There was a risk of a horrible mix-up, especially when we were both playing grayling at the same time. But fortune was with us, and by the time the sun-lit patch had dwindled away to nothing, we were each very satisfied with our catches. And there had been no calamity.

The sunshine having gone, we thought that the grayling would probably move further up the pool and we certainly did not expect sport to end abruptly at that moment. But we both continued to fish hard until the light went and neither of us had another bite.

Some years earlier, I had a very different experience about 300 yards farther down the river. Alec Broadley, an old army colleague, joined me for a day's trotting. Conditions were quite arctic, with ice on the edge of the river, and when we started fishing a moderate east wind was tunnelling upstream. We tried several good swims, but had a lot of trouble with the rod rings freezing up and had no success. All the time the wind was steadily increasing in force and it was most terribly cold.

In those days, after the long wartime gap in my fishing activities, hardly anything but darkness could drive me from the river, and I continued fishing while Alec sheltered in a niche in the side of the limestone cliff. I ought to say, though, that the cold never troubles me apart from a tingle in the ears and the fingers when it is really bitter. However, I eventually found a shoal of grayling just round the corner from the pool at Loup Scaur. The swim was about three feet deep and the flow only fair. I landed five or six fish in very little time and then called Alec to come and take over. Unfortunately the icy wind was then getting up to gale force. What with the difficulty it caused in casting, the freezing up of the rod rings and the fact that Alec was in agony with the cold, he could do no good and retired again to his shelter.

Before I could restart fishing I had to suck the rod rings clear of ice and dry them thoroughly with the small hand towel I always carry. I thought it worthwhile, too, to rub my ears and fingers for a minute. Then, to my horror, I found my bag of gilt-tails was frozen hard. Rather despairingly, I broke off a piece of the rigid moss and extracted a waxy-looking gilt-tail, which I proceeded to thaw out between the palms of my hands. The thing was still utterly lifeless, but I put it on the hook and cast out. The fierce, upstream wind was making big waves and all my efforts to make the float travel with the flow were useless – the float remained in front of me, rising and falling with the waves. This seemed a hopeless situation and I was about to reel up and call it a day, when I noticed that the float had not risen again on the wave as it ought to have done. I struck rather automatically and was amazed to find that it was, in fact, a grayling that had taken. The net, too was frozen solid, but I managed with it and held the fish up for Alec to see.

The return of the line through the rod rings while playing the fish resulted in the icing-up again. I dealt with this, and my ears and fingers; thawed out another gilt-tail, and cast out again. Within seconds the float failed to rise with the wave again and another grayling was landed. The whole sequence of laborious little jobs was repeated time after time. The grayling must have been most dreadfully hungry, because I never had to wait for more than a few seconds before one was hooked. But the float never went under from the top of a wave like a normal bite. Every time it simply failed to rise again with the wave.

The grayling were still active when ultimately I stopped fishing, which was largely for Alec's sake. When we counted up at the car, I was annoyed that I had not stayed for one more grayling – the catch numbered 19!

I must say quite frankly that now being another 20 years older, I am no longer willing to subject myself to such trials. I am still always anxious to find the grayling in arctic conditions, but once a shoal has been located and two or three fish landed, my ambition for that day is satisfied.

A much more pleasant day on the Wharfe a few years ago brought a memorable event for me. It was early December and my companion was Herbert Normington, a very experienced game fisher and at that time the president of the Burnsall Club.

It was close on noon when we parked close to the river, so we decided to fish for a while and return to the car for lunch. I started in a favourite glide near the tail of a long, deepish pool. Herbert said he would go to the top of the pool and fish the several good swims on the way down again.

The sky was dull and without a break, but there was hardly any wind and it was not at all cold. I saw no reason why my swim should not live up to its splendid reputation, but I covered all the lies very carefully without the float ever showing even a tremble. Eventually a few duns floated down and when I saw them sail out of view without being touched, I realised that either there were no grayling in the pool, or they were in a very dour frame of mind. Soon afterwards, Herbert arrived back with exactly the same story to tell. We left the river feeling rather perplexed.

Lunch out of the way, we considered driving further up the river, but decided that we could probably do no better than try the same pool again. We felt certain that there were bound to be fish there, and if they were completely off the feed, it was unlikely that things would be different elsewhere.

Back on the river, I decided to fish my swim of the morning's effort before going upstream, and Herbert said he would have a few casts immediately above while waiting for me.

My first trot produced a grayling of a little under a pound: the second and third did likewise. Herbert came down and stood beside me and the next two or three trots each succeeded in taking grayling, all of a similar weight. We then continued to count carefully to see how long the sequence of a grayling for every trot would last.

In ten consecutive casts, I had ten grayling. The eleventh trot failed to produce a bite, so I had one more throw to see what would happen and another grayling was brought to the net. Then I handed over to Herbert and the sport continued, a bite coming practically every other trot.

After a while, I left Herbert and tried the excellent water both above and below him, but could not get a single bite. It was clear that the entire shoal was concentrated in the one swim close to a little group of trees on the bank. Having satisfied myself on this point, I settled down to enjoy watching Herbert being kept very busy indeed. He suggested that I should take over again, but for me the pleasure of that day was already well beyond being improved upon. I was most happy to continue netting grayling for Herbert until the light went and he could see his float no more.

A more recent episode took place on a chalk stream when I was the guest of Arthur Oglesby for a day's trotting.

For a long time we covered lots of eminently suitable water, leapfrogging from pool to pool; but apart from the odd trout, neither of us got an offer. Eventually, on one of the occasions when I was ahead of Arthur, I thought I saw a rise on a bend in the river a good distance in front of me. A careful watch confirmed it: there was another, this time unmistakable, rise, and I hurried to the spot. Soon there were three or four grayling on the bank. Arthur arrived; and as lunch was considerably overdue, he watched while having a bite to eat and then took over while I lunched. There was all the evidence needed that this small dub – if I dare call a little, deepish hole on a chalk stream by that name – was densely populated with very hungry grayling.

Having eaten, I left Arthur and went to see what could be found in similar swims ahead. There were what seemed to be perfect places every 50 or 60 yards, and I fished a good number of them very hopefully. But it was no use. I hooked a few splendid rainbows and one very big brownie, and that was all.

Arthur was still catching grayling when I got back to him. We then shared the small swim, which meant only a very short trotting distance each, but it made no difference – both floats kept on being pulled under.

Once or twice there were spells when the grayling seemed to go a little cautious and there were touches that were missed. However, although there were 45 fewer grayling in that little corner when darkness began to creep in not much after three o'clock, enough offers were still coming to show that the shoal had not lost an important part of its number.

Brief Mentions

1. Selection of Method

Most fly fishers choose to delay their long-trotting until the colder weather when prospects with the fly become less promising. There are, however, some notable exceptions – experts with the fly who say that they enjoy trotting so much, in its own right as well as a change from fly fishing, that they look first for opportunities for float fishing for grayling and only resort to the fly when conditions offer no real choice.

Yet no matter which style of fishing is given priority, it is very frustrating to find when on the river that the equipment to hand is patently wrong for the ruling circumstances.

On chalk streams there is no problem if the rule is dry-fly and nymph only. The same rod, reel and line being suitable for both methods, it only takes a couple of minutes to change over from one to the other. The experienced angler who may be keenest to hook the bigger specimens will probably concentrate on the nymph. The novice or stranger to the water, however, will usually have the easiest chance of sport with the dry-fly for as far into the season as there are reasonable patches of duns.

In calm weather on the chalk stream when at least a few natural flies are about, the finding of the fish could not be easier. A few rises on a stretch of water that has never been seen before is all that is needed. My first ever visits for dry-fly fishing for grayling on two widely separated chalk streams each produced a basket of well into the teens, although in both cases the effective fishing period was relatively short due to the hospitality of hosts and such like diversions. During the actual fishing, sport could hardly have been faster and anyone who can put a fly on the water passably well would have been kept very busy.

At the same time, in calm weather one should always be on the watch for those occasions when visibility into the water is particularly good. This can happen with various kinds of overhead conditions and usually does not last very long. It is very nice during such periods, of course, to watch the grayling come up from the bottom to take the dry-fly, but many anglers think it wiser not to miss the excellent opportunity to do some visual nymph fishing.

The absence of surface fly on the chalk stream does not necessarily mean that the dry artificial will not be successful. But if there is the combination of no fly and more than the slightest bit of breeze, it will probably pay to settle for nymph fishing until a change in conditions suggests otherwise. If the gilt-tail is permitted, of course, it kills very well. And due to the relatively constant level of the water, the pools that make good swims for trotting can be relied upon to be fishable infinitely more than those on rain-fed rivers. If poor weather for fly fishing occurs early on in the grayling season, it is very satisfactory to be able to take the trotting tackle to a chalk stream and know that there will be no worry about the river being too big to fish.

The rain-fed rivers vary very considerably in respect of the methods of fishing that the different heights of water will allow to be done reasonably well. Generally speaking, the larger the river, the better it is able to carry extra water without interfering too much with the scope for effective fishing with either fly or trotting tackle. It is chiefly a question of the speed of the surface flow. A small spate probably means nothing more than the grayling having to move a little nearer the side to find the sort of current that is to their liking. In that case, the decision whether to use fly or bait tackle will depend simply on the overhead conditions.

On smaller streams, especially those stretches with high banks that confine the pools to a constant width, it requires very little rise in the water to spoil the chance to do any fly fishing, while quite a small spate may make it hopeless even for trotting.

On the other hand, the smaller streams drop back to a nice fishing level very quickly indeed. It is not unusual to find the water too high to fish in the morning, and yet be catching grayling by the afternoon. The larger rivers run off much more slowly, and once they reach a height that makes fishing impossible, it may be a day or two before there is any worthwhile improvement.

Familiarity with the way the rain-fed rivers behave in relation to the immediate weather is essential, both for selecting which one of these – if there is any choice – will offer the best prospects on the particular day, and for deciding which method will probably be the most suitable.

No matter how sound the basis of judgment may be, however, sudden changes in the weather can produce excellent chances of sport for which one is not correctly equipped. The only real answer to the problem would be a rod that would give a good performance in long-trotting and also throw a fly line reasonably well.

In fibre-glass, it should be possible to produce a very light, quick action rod of about 10 foot 6 inches that would be a reasonably good compromise.

The stiffness wanted for trotting would be moderated

by the weight of the fly line, and very probably it would be nicer for wet-fly than a lot of the short dry-fly rods that are commonly made to do the work these days. It could not be expected to throw a dry-fly a long distance accurately, but that is not very important. Accuracy to fine limits is not needed, and more grayling are caught on dry-fly with very moderate casts than at long range. The rod would require double rings – the ones for the float line mounted on top of those for the fly line – but this should not result in any practical disadvantage. Also the reel fittings would need to be of the universal type.

The additional weight requiring to be carried in order to provide for the change-over from trotting to fly fishing or vice versa would be of no consequence – probably less than one pound. But the additional weight of fish that might have to be carried as a result of it could be considerable. Certainly a successful dual purpose rod would be a boon to the grayling fisher.

2. *Response of the grayling*

The activities of a trout in prime condition are governed almost exclusively by the availability of food and the capacity of the fish to continue feeding.

Such factors are only part of the story with grayling. After a very quiet period, they frequently become responsive to the angler's lure when there is no evidence of any change in their prospects of finding natural food.

So far I have approached the grayling problem on the basis of the angler's acceptance of the apparent simple facts and his attempts to cope with them at their face value. The scope for speculation, however, concerning the reasons for some of the unpredictable and inexplicable behaviour of the fish is very intriguing.

Perhaps there is little hope of discovering anything

which could be of useful, practical application, over and above what has already been said. Nevertheless, any study that gives a fuller understanding of the grayling can assuredly add to the pleasure of observing any activity which takes place and which has probably been hoped for, but could not have been anticipated on a calculated basis.

Certain comparisons can help in the review of the question. The difference in behaviour between the grayling and the brown trout make certain similarities between the grayling for the one part and salmon and sea trout for the other part, very much more notable. In normal water conditions that can be assumed to be reasonably comfortable for the fish, salmon, sea trout and grayling share the habit of always lying close to the bottom and if they rise and take a small item on or close to the surface, they return immediately to their lies on the bottom. Also, all three kinds of fish lie dormant for periods, and on some occasions when there is virtually nothing happening in their environment to excite them and cause any dramatic change of mood, they suddenly become very responsive to the lures of the angler.

This makes it clear that there must be some invisible physical influences, quite apart from the positive opportunity to feed, that can put the grayling into a humour that will make sport possible. I do not wish here to involve the reader in the subject of the chemistry of the water, and will confine my observations to the simple truth that changes in the overhead conditions are quite as capable of shaking the grayling out of a lethargic mood as is the appearance of a hatch of fly.

The real difficulty of the problem lies in the fact that the variety of changes in items of the weather that can bring about the desired improvement includes many opposites. For example, an increase or equally a reduction in the temperature, the borametric pressure, the relative humidity of the atmosphere, the amount of wind or the amount of sunshine, can each be responsible for putting the grayling into a responsive mood.

The complexity of the alternatives suggests that only one inference can be drawn. It is that if conditions are very stable and the grayling are showing no interest, any change at all in overhead conditions may have the possibility of bringing about the desired improvement. Any such change in the weather has its influence on the state of the water as it affects the fish. Some of the changes will be for the better and some will be for the worse – one cannot judge – but the chance of an improvement at any time may only be a few minutes away.

Fortunately, it so happens in seasonable weather during the grayling months that any stable conditions are usually favourable for sport. It is the noticeably 'wrong' weather that is mostly poor for fishing. For instance, a raw day in October with the weather coming from the east would not be considered to be promising. Then, if the breeze were to drop and some sunshine made it feel a little less chilly, there would be good hopes of the grayling coming on to the take. On the other hand, anti-cyclonic conditions in October with very dry air and a lot of sunshine would probably result in a complete lack of sport during the middle of the day. But as the temperature dropped in the late afternoon, the grayling would probably become very active.

During the autumn and winter, of course, a lot of mixed and changeable weather is to be expected, and then it would be very much guesswork to say what was wanted to bring about the end of a spell of poor sport. I remember one day in particular when I was wishing that the sun would break through and liven up the grayling. Instead, a heavy flurry of snow came. It was almost blinding and I could hardly see the float, but bites came rapidly at close quarters and the sport was hectic.

As I have suggested before, the only thing to do is to fish on and be thankful that the grayling do not usually remain uncooperative for very long. Nevertheless, there is no harm in watching the details of the weather in the hope that eventually a helpful pattern might emerge.

Another point deserves comment before leaving the question of the differences and similarities between the grayling and other game fish, because the close similarities seem quite extraordinary. Since the grayling is subject to the same overall environmental influences as the brown trout, and there is no genetical difference between the brown trout and the sea trout, it would seem that all three fish should adopt the same behaviour when feeding on the surface. It would not seem very surprising if the brown trout and the sea trout behaved alike and the grayling differently. But the fact that the grayling and the sea trout share the same habit, and the brown trout has its own individual method, poses a problem. It is a reasonable assumption that the brown trout's method of remaining close to the surface and taking flies in rapid succession is the most efficient for it, giving the best return for the energy expended. But also it must be remembered that when the feast is over, the brown trout usually moves away to a comfortable, easy and secure lie elsewhere; whereas the sea trout and grayling tend to remain in the same position on the bottom (in the daytime), whether or not there are any flies to be had on the surface.

A possible solution to the problem may be suggested, therefore, if the reason can be found for the sea trout's departure from what must be assumed to be its original, hereditary type of behaviour when surface feeding. If the water is at a suitable level for running, the sea trout is often thus engaged, especially during the night, and then, of course, it is near the surface all the time. When it is not running, it prefers to remain close to the bottom, where it is more unobtrusive. Also, the temperature of the water usually being fairly high, it favours a strong flow provided there is enough depth to give it satisfactory cover. Furthermore, food in fresh water is a very secondary matter to the sea trout – it can well do without it. When, however, the sea trout does rise to take the occasional fly, it drops back to the bottom again immediately. In the circumstances, it is clearly more economical for it to employ that practice than the one used by the brown trout. In other words, the priorities of the sea trout are different and adherence to these creates the need for other variations in behaviour as compared with the brown trout.

Now it can possibly be seen why the grayling's behaviour is so similar to that of the sea trout. Firstly there is the matter of security from the menace of the trout. To remain for any length of time near the surface would leave it too exposed, and the lie close to the bottom is the best possible protection. Secondly, the trout take the easiest and most profitable feeding lies, leaving for the grayling only the ones requiring the hardest work and smallest return. Bearing in mind the rate at which the grayling gets the flies and the effort incurred, its method is fairly certain to be the most economical in its case, too, besides being the most prudent. No doubt this is the reason why the grayling favours relatively shallow water during the part of the season when good hatches of fly can be expected.

3. The Grayling's Vision

Discussions about the sight of the grayling are often to be heard and are taken very seriously. Opinions vary from believing that it is exceptionally keen to considering it to be very much inferior to that of the trout.

I support the view that the important question is not how well the fish can see, but how much of that which is seen registers sufficiently to be of any influence.

The grayling can undoubtedly see the tiniest specks of insects and it is most unlikely that the cast and the exposed part of the hook fail to be seen. But so long as their appearance, along with everything else that forms part of the general image, is within a certain margin of tolerance, the fish disregards them. Thus, when the lure creates its impression as an item of food, what is seen of the cast and hook does not detract from the impulse of the fish to take. Experience in any kind of game fishing soon establishes good indications of the margins of tolerance that will permit sport. These tolerances also apply, of course, to numerous other matters, such as the way the lure looks and behaves, and the various factors involved in presentation. For example, in most dry-fly fishing for trout, the margin of tolerance concerning drag is practically nil. If there is a good hatch of one specific type of dun, the margin of tolerance in the dressing of the artificial can be quite small. In much of the dry-fly fishing for grayling, the margin of tolerance in respect of the components of the dressing is remarkably wide.

In grayling fishing generally, the narrowest margins of tolerance are those concerning the size of the fly or bait, and the thickness of the cast. It is quite clear that three lb nylon; small, sparsely dressed flies on size 16 hooks and smaller; and gilt-tail worms, are all reasonably safely within the tolerances. If one finds sport very difficult when other rods are catching grayling, those are the primary items in which a mistake is likely to be found.

When a grayling misses a dry-fly several times, I do not think it is accidental, due to poor sight, as some anglers contend. Nor do I think it is because the nylon has put the fish off, as others argue. When feeding on natural duns, a grayling seldom fails to get the fly, which shows that all the senses are adequate and perfectly well coordinated. If the nylon were responsible for making the fish hesitate and fail to get the artificial, why should it ultimately ignore the nylon? A 'gut-shy' fish is more likely to become more obstinate and not less wary.

What seems to me to be the reasonable answer is that the dry-fly makes the initial impression that it might be an item of food and the grayling does not pay any attention to the nylon although it actually sees it. But unless the fish is either very hungry or is fully deceived by the artificial, something to do with the actual dressing deters it at the last moment. However, after a few casts and repeated examinations of the fly, familiarity with its appearance and faults makes the grayling less suspicious and the temptation of food to be had then dominates. Or it could be put another way. It is generally agreed that fish cannot be credited with any powers of reasoning. They respond to impressions, reflexes and impulses. If the impression and the impulse are there – as must be so if the grayling approaches the fly several times – whatever the nature of the deterrent from taking might be, it must be very marginal. It is not surprising, therefore, that ultimately it is ignored and the fly is taken.

Smutting grayling that persistently refuse to look at the artificial can also make one wonder if the cast is too noticeable. In some lights, it is not impossible for that to be the trouble, of course; but most experiences suggest otherwise.

Frequently the refusal is eventually followed by a hatch of duns. Then the grayling feed and take the appropriate artificial as would be expected. This makes one wonder if the fish can sense that a hatch of duns is due.

I am always pleased if smutting fish can be coaxed

into taking, but not disappointed if they ignore my efforts, since this can be the cue that something even better is in prospect. And when the grayling persist in proving that they are more than a match for the tackle and my performance with it, I remain confident that only time is needed to bring a change in my favour. My very high opinion of the powers of vision of the grayling gives me no fear concerning the outcome of an imminent new kind of encounter.

4. Stocks of Grayling

So much restocking and hatchery work is done with trout that it is impossible to relate the stocks at any one time in many rivers with the degree to which natural spawning was successful during the preceding two or three years. With grayling, it may be very different. Some seasons there are remarkably big stocks of one particular size of fish. Other years grayling in general seem to be rather scarce and no one size of fish predominates. This suggests that from time to time there is an exceptionally successful spawning season, and on other occasions results are very much below average.

When grayling are very prolific there is a tendency for some anglers to be apprehensive that the trout stocks are bound to suffer seriously. This threat is unlikely to be as dangerous as it seems. Granted that there are some exceptions, the majority of grayling do not survive for more than five or six years. The result is that the big stock seems to dwindle very quickly, and within a few seasons, the worry may well be the other way round. On many rivers where no removal of grayling by netting is ever done, the relative stocks of trout and grayling over the years stay within the same reasonable limits of variation. Certainly the grayling never seem to get the upper hand as some anglers fear will happen.

Non-grayling fishers sometimes assert that if the grayling were removed from a river, the trout would be bigger, fatter and more numerous: they regard that opinion as being incontestable. I should prefer to avoid this particular subject, because as a sincere supporter of the fostering of all game fishing interests, I do not wish my esteem of the grayling to be imagined to involve any prejudice against the trout. Nevertheless, it must be said that most of the blame that is put on the grayling in this connection is quite unreasonable.

First look at any chalk stream in which there is an abundance of food. Both trout and grayling can often be seen lying dormant when there are plenty of flies to be had. Clearly there is more than enough food for all the fish. But they need time as well as food to grow big and fat. If the grayling tend to be bigger than the trout, it is because the trout are caught and taken before they have had a chance to grow bigger, not because they are underfed. And the grayling are not bigger through taking the food that is needed by the trout, but because fewer anglers fish for them and they remain in the water to feed for a longer period. If all the grayling could be removed, it would probably not make the slightest difference to the average size of the trout, even in the long term. The truth about good chalk streams is that they are expected by some anglers to produce a larger number of bigger trout per season than the time factor will permit. If the position were remedied by closing the water for two years, the improved standard would be unlikely to last much more than one season.

Insufficient food for the trout may be the reason for their small size in stony rain-fed rivers that tend slightly towards acidity. It may seem to be wrong at first, but the probability is that the presence or otherwise of grayling makes practically no difference to the trout. The trouble is that the food is restricted almost entirely to aquatic flies. When there is a good hatch, all the fish feed as fast as they can, but they only get a small proportion of the flies, and there are plenty left for the birds and for breeding stocks. If a single trout were the sole inhabitant of the river, it would probably not get many more flies during the hatch than it manages to do in apparent competition with a great number of other fish. The trouble is not the competition, but the fact that the opportunities to feed do not occur with the frequency that would be needed to produce a better average size.

On rain-fed rivers where there are no grayling, the average size of the trout is no better than in similar waters which contain good stocks of grayling. And there has been little or no difference over the years. All the evidence shows that any particular type of river can only maintain a certain maximum average size of trout whether they be few or many, and whether or not grayling are present. If the stocks of trout are smaller in average size than the water is capable of producing, the blame must be put squarely on the angler and not on the grayling.

If there were any substance in the accusations against the grayling there would be no problem in increasing the average size of the trout in enclosed waters and those rivers where there are no grayling. But the absence of grayling does not remove the problem and undoubtedly the vital factor everywhere is whether or not the water is over-fished for the trout.

I, for one, believe the grayling to be innocent.

5. The Angler and the Grayling

In 1966 Arthur Oglesby caught a bigger number of salmon – best fish 46½ lb – than the season's catch of many a trout fisher who neither covets salmon nor 'bothers' with grayling. Yet as soon as autumn came, Arthur was enthusiastically going about his grayling fishing, like lots of other expert game fishers up and down the country.

My mention of this is not in the way of making a plea on behalf of the standing of the grayling: it is to show that no such plea is necessary.

Nothing in the character and dignity of a member of the salmon family is lacking in the grayling. It is not, however, the grayling's relationship with the salmon and the trout that qualifies it as a game fish. The versatile way in which it fills the gap in autumn and winter with sport to fly and bait entitles it to this distinction in its own right.

The grayling has long been known as 'The Lady of the Stream'. From an artistic or poetic point of view, this is a very apt name and far be it from me to be critical of intended compliments to the grayling. Yet to do the grayling full justice, any mention of it should make one mindful of the virility and the toughness needed for it to be in its prime when so much else in nature is sheltering, if not dormant or in hibernation.

My theme earlier was that it says a lot for the fish if you look at the kind of angler who goes in search of the grayling. I hope the reader will be of the opinion also that the reversal of the commendation is a pleasant truth.

Appendix A

Relative Lengths and Weights of Grayling

Terry Thomas has spent a lot of time investigating and studying the question of the natural distribution of grayling. This is complicated by the fact that grayling have been introduced successfully into quite a number of rivers: it is therefore difficult to be certain that the fish in any river are truly indigenous.

One discussion with Terry prompted me to ask Leslie Stewart, the Fishery Officer of the Lancashire River Authority, why the river Lune virtually has no grayling (I have seen only one) when its neighbour, the Ribble, contains a thriving population. Leslie's explanation was that grayling never do well in water that has a tendency to be acid, and the more alkaline the river, the more suitable it is for the general needs of the grayling. The following figures bear this out fully.

*Weights of Grayling Measuring 14 inches
from nose to fork of tail*

Wharfe		15½ oz	Yorkshire		
Tweed	1lb		Derwent	1lb	3½ oz
Ribble	1lb	2½ oz	Wylye	1lb	6 oz

Lengths of grayling weighing one lb

Wharfe	14½ inches	Ribble	13½ inches
Tweed	14 inches	Yorkshire	
		Derwent	13 inches

Oliver Kite kindly provided me with the figures for the Wylye, and said that the little River Till, a narrow and fairly shallow tributary of the Wylye, produces the heaviest grayling relative to their length in his neighbourhood. The diet is chiefly shrimp. He mentioned having caught a number of grayling in the Till of 1 lb 15 oz that measured almost exactly 16 inches, while one of a fraction under 16 inches weighed 1 lb 15½ oz. A 16 inch fish I caught on the Ribble, which looked very fat indeed, weighed 1 lb 10¾ oz. The Till fish must undoubtedly be among the absolute leaders in the weight/length comparisons.

During the winter of 1965/66, a grayling of 2 lbs 1½ oz which measured 17 inches was caught on the upper Yorkshire Derwent. Fish of these proportions are not common, but the few that are taken from time to time confirm that the Derwent is most excellently suited to the needs of the grayling.

Comparisons in photographs of the very slender grayling from the shallow, stony rivers and those from waters with lush feed, may give a wrong impression. It may be thought that the slender type looks undernourished and poor. That is not so at all. The intestines and various organs in such fish are a very small proportion of the weight, which is mainly composed of very firm, thick flesh. The smaller girth is mostly a matter of less depth – the thickness of the body is very good. Such a fish looks and indeed probably is in all respects exactly as nature intends it to be in the circumstances. One's eye gets attuned to the proportions, with the result that it is the portly grayling that tends to look too fat, rather than the slender one looking thin.

Appendix B

Making a Grayling Float

Balsa Wood in ⅜ inch square strips and 20 gauge piano wire are required. Model-making shops usually have these in stock.

Figures 1 to 5 show the float at all stages of production.

The most useful size for the body is about 3½ inches. The wood is shaped as in Fig. 2 with a sharp knife. It is then held in fine sandpaper between the thumb and forefinger of the left hand, and twisted with the thumb and forefinger of the right hand. This quickly smooths the soft wood and makes it symetrical. Now a small hole is made in the base with a darning needle as a starter to take the stem.

The wire for the stem is cut to about 1 inch longer than the body of the float (Fig. 3). The stem is held vertically on a hard surface, and using the starter hole, the body is pressed down on the stem. Not much pressure is needed to make the wire penetrate to a depth of about one inch. During this process care must be taken to ensure that the body and stem are kept in correct line so that the stem does not finish up at an angle to the body. When the stem is properly home, the exposed part should be approximately the same length as the body.

Now with the float at the stage shown in Fig. 4, the base of the body is whittled down until the wood is flush with the stem (Fig 5). The fine wire loop is whipped on to the base of the stem and the float is ready for its first coat of paint.

The white cellulose paint or dope undercoat can be put on the wood thickly, because a lot of it is absorbed. It appears to dry very quickly – in about a quarter of an hour – but it is best to leave it for several hours. The wood is then whiskery. It is smoothed off with fine sandpaper and this leaves the surface of the wood quite hard and ready for the next coat.

Green cellulose paint is applied to all the float excepting the antenna, which is left white to take the fluorescent red. If the fluorescent paint is applied thickly enough for one coat to be sufficient, it takes much too long to dry properly, if it ever does so. Terry Thomas made enquiries from the makers and their advice was to put on several very thin coats, each one being allowed to dry before the next one is applied. This has proved to be a very satisfactory method and the fluorescent colour is certainly well worth the trouble.

Richard Walker has kindly given me the following recommendations for producing a finish that is very resistant to deterioration:

For piano wire, substitute beryllium copper or hard nickel silver. These wires will not rust, are very springy, and as they are a little heavier than steel, No. 22 s.w.g. is about the right size for the dimension of float mentioned above. Crimp the end of the wire, push it into the wood, withdraw it, coat it with Araldite, and replace it in the wood. This gives a very secure hold. Then to waterproof the balsa, heat it almost to the point of scorching and plunge it into a can of cellulose varnish, where it must remain submerged for two hours. Paint applied after this treatment will not crack. One thin coat of fluorescent paint gives the best results in respect of being seen at

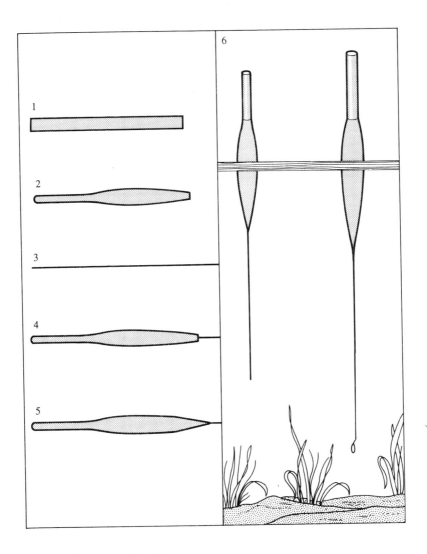

1–5 Making a grayling float.
6 Grayling floats without shot. Suitable shotting lowers the floats so that only the antennae are above the surface.

a great distance. If thought necessary, apply a coat of clear varnish over the fluorescent paint.

Lastly, always remember to make plenty of spares, because your friends will give you no peace until they get their share. If you are so thoughtless as to fail to make enough, you will be the one who has to do without. Please don't ask me how many is enough – I have never yet found out.

Appendix C

Gathering and Keeping Gilt-Tails

A heap of lawn mowings at a bowling green or park is usually a good and easy source of supply of gilt-tails. The worms will be in the dampest place where the heap has been undisturbed for a long time and the cuttings have rotted down well. One turn of a fork in a good place will expose enough gilt-tails for a day's fishing. However, it is as well to get all you can when they are available because they are quite easy to keep in good trim throughout the winter.

A cotton bag is the best container. Put in an ample supply of clean, damp Sphagnum Moss. The gilt-tails will collect in the middle where the moisture is retained the best and they will not try to escape. Of course, when not in use, the mouth of the bag should be tied up with the tape.

Be sure not to hang the bag up where a draught can dry out the moss or cause it to freeze. Some evaporation will occur, of course, wherever the bag is stored. It requires to be examined periodically and a little water added when necessary.

Once a week pour two tablespoonfuls of the top of the milk into the moss. The gilt-tails will consume the lot and there is no need to fear that the moss will turn foul.

If gilt-tails are scoured too much they go thin, pale and lifeless. The diet suggested keeps them more or less at their best. When starting with a new supply however, you will find them quite suitable for use immediately without any scouring having taken place. They may be a little soft and easier to throw off the hook, but the grayling like them just as much, if not better.

It is a good plan to get a colony of gilt-tails established in a corner of the garden, but one warning is necessary. Bernard Venables wanted to do this and when he failed to find the starting supply. I sent him a good tinful. He dug a good-sized hole under some trees where evaporation would not be too fast and filled it with rotted grass and leaf mould. He introduced the gilt-tails to this perfect home and left nature to do its work. Occasionally he took a look to see that the leaf mould was moist enough, but otherwise left it undisturbed.

Eventually the day came when Bernard wanted his first bag of gilt-tails. He started turning over the leaf mould, but after a very thorough search, not a worm was to be found. Then he noticed many little bore-holes leading away from the earth sides. That was the answer. Moles are just as fond of gilt-tails as the grayling are.

Appendix D

Grayling for the Table

Before the war a famous fruit, fish and game shop in Bradford often used to display a dishful of grayling. I forget the exact wording, but a label said in effect that the fish were from Kelso, where they had been netted from the River Tweed. The grayling were regarded as a delicacy and found a ready sale.

Grayling never taste muddy and this is perhaps one reason why many people who are not particularly keen on trout are always appreciative of grayling. I know nothing about cooking, but the important thing seems to be that the grayling should not be underdone. When correctly cooked, the flesh is firm and there is no difficulty in avoiding bones. I cannot imagine that anyone who likes fish would not find grayling to be very pleasant eating indeed.

As with all freshwater fish, grayling should be cooked as fresh as ever possible. It is a mistake ever to put them in a refrigerator. An expert in the freezing of food once told me that the slow reduction in temperature in a refrigerator separates certain fluids from the flesh of fish and these form into small frozen globules. When the temperature is raised again, the fluids remain separate and the result is that the cooked fish is of a poor consistency and flavour. Quick, deep freezing, he said, was different. The flesh undergoes no physical change and when thawed out again, it is in the same state as before the freezing.

My own experience confirms this and it now seems to me to be a crime to put any game fish in the refrigerator. Of course, if the fish has previously been deep-frozen and not properly thawed out, the refrigerator is a satisfactory means of keeping it. However, the real charm of the grayling is lost unless it is eaten as soon as possible after it has been taken from the river.

Index